JavaScript Native Interface

Tony Gaitatzis

BackupBrain Publishing, 2022

eBook ISBN: 978-1-989775-19-6

Paperback ISBN: 978-1-989775-18-9

backupbrain.co

JavaScript Native Interface

by Tony Gaitatzis

Dedication

To Christofer, for inspiring me to solve problems

Table of Contents

JavaScript Interface

Introduction

JavaScript Interface (JSI) offers developers to the convenience of cross-platform apps with the performance of native apps.

It lets developers to write functions in C++ that can be called directly from JavaScript, for example in a React Native front-end. It works by combining two existing features of React Native:

1. The native code (for example Swift or Java) can call binary functions from compiled C++

2. React Native JavaScript can call properly-defined native functions

C++ code can be written in a cross-platform way and compiled for a variety of devices, such as Android and iOS, as long as it doesn't work on device-specific or platform-specific features such as user interfaces or certain hardware such as sensors or specific camera features.

Since both the JavaScript and C++ are cross-platform and the native layer can bind these languages together, it is possible to create React Native apps for several platforms with one code base.

Javascript Native Interface code must be written so that functions and data types are compatible with the JavaScript type system, and those functions must be properly exported to the JavaScript environment.

This book will walk you through understanding how to set up a React Native project to use JSI, and how to implement common function types in JSI, including those that take or return arrays and complex object types, Promises, and multi-threaded functions.

1

What is JavaScript Native Interface

JavaScript Interface (JSI) is a lightweight, general-purpose API provided by Facebook for interacting with JavaScript data types and functions in C++ code. Introduced in the context of React Native, JSI offers a way to call C++ functions directly from JavaScript and vice versa.

Before JSI, React Native used a "Native Bridge" feature, which required that developers write native code in the device-native language, for example Swift on iOS and Java or Kotlin on Android. React Native developers who wanted to have the performance of a native app therefore needed to maintain two code-bases for the same features. JSI solves this by allowing developers to maintain high-performance code in only one language: C++.

While JSI brings numerous advantages, especially for complex and performance-critical applications, it's worth noting that it requires a good understanding of both C++ and JavaScript, as well as the internals of React Native. As such, it's often used for building advanced features, or optimizing performance-critical paths.

JSI is evolving as part of React Native's architecture, with ongoing efforts to leverage its capabilities for enhancing the framework's performance and developer experience. As such, JSI has an evolving set of features and best practices, making it more challenging to work with than typical JavaScript-only or Native Bridge applications.

Why It Was Created

JSI addresses fundamental limitations in React Native's original architecture, particularly the inefficiencies of the bridge mechanism that facilitated communication between JavaScript and native code. Traditionally, this bridge relied on serializing data into a JSON-like format to pass messages, a process that introduced significant overhead, especially for operations requiring frequent or complex data exchanges. This serialization not only slowed down performance but also made synchronous calls between JavaScript and native layers cumbersome, limiting the types of interactions and optimizations developers could implement.

By enabling direct and type-safe interactions between JavaScript and C++ without serialization, JSI significantly reduces this overhead, offering a pathway to both improved performance and synchronous execution capabilities. This solves critical performance bottlenecks, simplifies the development of high-performance native modules, and supports a more flexible and efficient integration of JavaScript with native code. Additionally, JSI's engine-agnostic API lays a foundation for future advancements in React Native, facilitating new features like TurboModules and the Fabric renderer that aim to enhance React Native's performance, startup times, and developer experience.

Take for example the speed difference between two libraries, Async Storage and MMKV. Both are in-memory key/value store databases for React Native, but Async Storage is written in JavaScript and MMKV is written in C++ for JavaScript Native Interface. This difference results in MMKV having a twenty times performance increase over Async Storage[1].

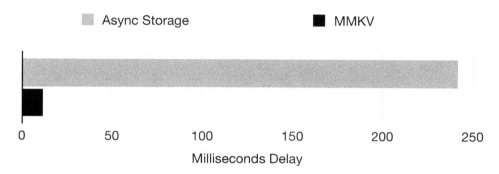

Figure 1.1: MMKV vs AsyncStorage time in executing 1000 requests

[1] Rousavy, Marc, et al. "Mrousavy/React-Native-Mmkv: the Fastest Key/Value Storage for React Native. ~30x Faster than AsyncStorage!" StorageBenchmark, 11 Jan. 2024, github.com/mrousavy/StorageBenchmark.

How it Works

JSI introduces a set of C++ classes and methods that represent JavaScript entities like values, objects, functions, and arrays. For instance, through JSI, a C++ function can be exposed to JavaScript as as though it were defined in JavaScript. Conversely, JSI allows native code to call JavaScript functions directly. This bidirectional interaction enables a seamless integration of native and JavaScript code.

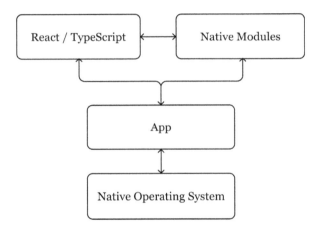

Figure 1.2: Simplified React Native architecture

Examples of JSI Projects

There are several popular React Native projects that leverage JSI for enhanced performance or capabilities.

- **Hermes**
  hermesengine.dev
  Hermes is the default JavaScript engine used by React Native. It's fast, has a quick start-up time, and a smaller memory footprint than the JavaScriptCore engine.

- **Reanimated2**
  docs.swmansion.com/react-native-reanimated
  Reanimated2 is an animation library for React Native. It uses JSI for smooth, native-like animations by running them on the UI thread, reducing overhead and enhancing responsiveness.

- **React Native Vision Camera**
  react-native-vision-camera.com
  An developer-friendly library that provides full control over camera features with great error handling and native-speeds.

These projects are at the core of a lot of other React Native Projects to varying degrees, so you are already using JSI perhaps without even realizing it.

Using Javascript Native Interface

To use JavaScript Native Interface, you must create a C++ file that will get compiled with your React Native project.

This C++ file will have a function describing which custom native functions will be available to JavaScript. This function is the JSI equivalent of the main() function of a standalone C program.

Unlike main(), this function can be given any name. But generally developers like to call it something that implies it's role of installing a module or library. It's job is to define the JSI functions and attach them to the JavaScript global context.

```
void installMyJsiModule(Runtime &runtime) {
  // native functions are defined in here
}
```

Sample 1.1: The main function of the JSI module

Inside this installer function, you must create a series of custom functions that you want to be available to your React Native Project. You do this by creating a new facebook::jsi::Function object like this:

```
Function myFunctionRef = Function::createHostFunction(...);
```

Sample 1.2: API call to create a JSI function

The `Function::createHostFunction()` function is important as it not only defines how your native function will execute, but also helps to give the function the name and describe its required arguments to TypeScript. It takes a few parameters:

Parameter	Explanation
`Runtime`	The React Native execution environment
`PropNameId`	The name of the function as seen in TypeScript
`unsigned int`	The number of parameters a function has
Lambda function	The function that will be executed by JavaScript

Table 1.1: Top level parameters of `Function::createHostFunction()`

The Lambda, or callback function is what actually gets executed by when calling the JSI function from TypeScript. This function is actually of type `Facebook::jsi::HostFunction`, which is why the function we are talking about is called `createFromHostFunction()`.

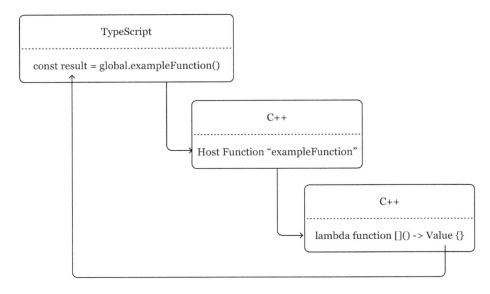

Figure 1.3: TypeScript calls a registered function which executes a lambda

The lambda function takes three parameters:

Parameter	Explanation
Runtime	The React Native execution environment
Value*	The pointer to the first element of a Value array
size_t	The number of arguments passed to the function

Table 1.2: Parameters of the lambda function within the `Function` *object*

Let's say we want to create a JSI function called myFunctionName() that takes two parameters. It could be defined like this:

```
void installExampleJsiLibrary(Runtime &runtime) {
  Function myFunctionRef = Function::createFromHostFunction(
  runtime,
  PropNameID::forAscii(runtime, "myFunctionName"),
  2,
  [](
    Runtime &runtime, const Value &thisValue,
    const Value *arguments,
    size_t count
  ) -> Value {
    // your logic goes here
  }
 );
}
```

Sample 1.3: Defining a JSI function

You can think of the installExampleJsiLibrary() function as working similar to a class, exposing methods to other parts of your software. Except the functions defined inside the installExampleJsiLibrary() are standalone functions with no need for instantiation. installExampleJsiLibrary() is a function that defines other functions rather than a class.

Although this is written in C++, if you are a TypeScript developer, it may be helpful to understand if you think of the C++ as working like this TypeScript code:

TypeScript

```
const myFunctionRef = createHostFunction(
  runtime,
  PropNameId.fromAscii(runtime, "myFunctionName"),
  0,
  (
    runtime: Runtime,
    thisValue: Value,
    count: int
  ) => Value {
  }
}
```

Sample 1.4: TypeScript version of the JSI host function signature

Now that your JSI function is defined, you must connect it to the React Native global context by using its .setProperty() method. This method takes the following parameters, like this:

C++

```cpp
void installExampleJsiLibrary(Runtime &runtime) {
  Function myFunctionRef = Function::createHostFunction(...);
  runtime.global().setProperty(
    runtime,
    "myFunctionName",
    move(myFunctionRef)
  );
}
```

Sample 1.5: Connecting the host function to React Native global context

The JSI Global.setProperty() method takes three parameters:

Parameter	Explanation
Runtime	The React Native execution environment
string*	The name of the function
Function*	The pointer to a facebook::jsi::Function

Table 1.3: Global.setProperty() function parameters

Together, these two steps will expose a myFunctionName() function in the React Native global scope with the following method signature:

TypeScript

```typescript
const myFunctionName = (param1: any, param2: any): void;
```

Sample 1.6: Calling the myFunctionName() JSI function from TypeScript

Since the method is accessible from the global scope, it can be called using JavaScript anywhere in a React Native component, fore example like this:

TypeScript JSX

```
export const ExampleComponent = () => {
  const onPress = () => {
    myFunctionName("param1", "param2");
  }
  return <Button title="Press" onPress={onPress} />
}
```

Sample 1.7: Calling the myFunctionName() function from React Native

The result is a function that's callable from JavaScript in React Native that executes with the speed of a native binary.

To better understand what the JSI is doing, it may be helpful to imagine how the equivalent logic might be written in TypeScript:

You can think of this code as working something like this TypeScript code:

TypeScript

```typescript
const installExampleJsiLibrary = () => {
  // describe a function
  const myFunctionRef = {
    name: "myFunctionName ",
    numArguments: 0,
    execute: (params: any): any => {
      // your logic goes here
    }
  }
  // link function execution to global context
  global["myFunctionName"] = myFunctionRef.execute;
}


// Called by another part of the program:
// installExampleLibrary();
// then global.myFunctionName() exists
```

Sample 1.8:Imagining JSI installation as a TypeScript method

2

Prepare Your Environment

Every development project requires its own tools. React Native requires coding C++ and TypeScript or Javascript, so it's important to have a code editor, a C compiler, and a JavaScript or TypeScript interpreter such as Node.js, as well as an emulator or simulator to test your software.

If you plan to develop for Android, you must install Android Studio, CMake, Android Native Development Kit (NDK), and an Android Emulator. If you plan to develop for iOS or MacOS, you must have a Mac computer with Xcode installed, as well as Ruby and CocoaPods.

Finally you'll need a code editor. The editor of choice for React Native developers tends to be Visual Studio (vscode) but of course you should use whatever editor makes you feel at home.

In summary, you will need:

- Node.js

- Visual Studio Code or some other code editor

- For Android Development:

  - Android Studio

  - Android Native Development Kit

  - An Android Emulator

  - CMake

- For iOS Development:

  - Xcode

  - Ruby

  - CocoaPods

Open source software projects are constantly changing. Small changes in these softwares can result in major issues for a developer, due to incompatibilities, poor documentation, bugs, or other issues. In order to have a stable development environment, it is important install and maintain versions that are known to work together.

This is especially important when working in cross-platform environments such as React Native and JavaScript Native Interface. Changes to the organization of header files on the host platform or compiler's libraries, deprecated configuration features, and other small changes can make it impossible to compile a React Native project with JSI.

At the time of this writing, the current working versions are React Native 0.74, Xcode 15 andAndroid Studio 2024.1.1 (Canary 8).

Install Node.js

Node.js is a free and open source JavaScript runtime environment essential for React Native development. It provides an environment for managing dependencies and executing JavaScript outside the browser, facilitating the build and testing of React Native applications.

At the time of writing, React Native requires NodeJS 18 or higher.

Install on MacOS

If you are using HomeBrew from brew.sh, the popular package manager for MacOS, you can install Node.js using the brew command:

Console

```
brew install nodejs
```

Example 2.1: Installing Node.js using Homebrew

Alternately you can download and install the latest version from the Node.js website, nodejs.org. Once downloaded, you can double-click the installer and follow the installation instructions.

Install on Windows

On Windows, you can download the latest version of Node.js from nodejs.org.

Once downloaded, double-click the installer file in your File Explorer to run it, and follow the on-screen instructions.

Install on Linux

Many Linux distributions have their own package management system which can install Node.js.

For example the Advanced Package Tool (APT) on Ubuntu and Debian systems:

Console

```
sudo apt update
sudo apt install nodejs npm
```

Example 2.2: Installing Node.js using apt on Linux

Fedora and RedHat Enterprise Linux systems use the Dandified YUM package manager:

Console

```
sudo dnf install nodejs
```

Example 2.3: Installing Node.js using yum on Linux

In any case, once Node.js is installed you make sure it works and is a useful version by running it from the command line:

```Console
node --version
```

Example 2.4: Get the version of the installed NodeJS program

Node.js should respond with text resembling the following:

```Console
v18.4.0
```

2.1: Example output of a NodeJS version

Install Android Development Kit

NDK is a toolset that lets you implement parts of your app using native-code languages such as C and C++. If you intend to develop React Native applications for Android devices such as phones, tablets, or Chromebook, you will need to install NDK.

In order to install NDK, you must first install Android Studio or your operating system by downloading it from developer.android.com/ studio. After running Android Studio, you can open the Tools menu, then open SDK Manager, switch to the SDK Tools tab. Look through the available tools to find NDK (Side by side) and check the box next to it. You may also want to check the boxes for CMake and LLB.

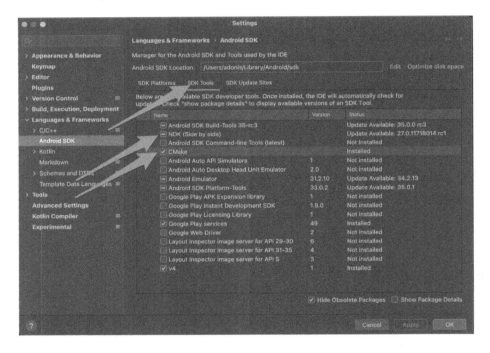

Figure 2.1: Installing NDK and CMake from Android Studio

Click OK to confirm your selection, and Android Studio will download and install the selected tools.

Installing CMake

CMake is a cross-platform, open source software for automation the building of other software. It lets developers build software for multiple platforms without needing to manually configure the build environment of each platform, by providing a simple language to get and set variables and configure compile and linking options in a single configuration file.

Installation on MacOS

If you are using HomeBrew, you can install CMake using the brew command:

Console

```
brew install cmake
```

Example 2.5: Installing cmake on MacOS using Homebrew

Alternately you can download and install the latest version from the CMake website, cmake.org. For most users that will be the macOS 10.13 universal disk image (dmg). Once downloaded you can double-click the install image and then run the following command in your Terminal:

Console

```
sudo "/Applications/CMake.app/Contents/bin/cmake-gui" --install
```

Example 2.6: Installing the cmake-gui on MacOS from Downloads

Installation on Windows

On Windows, you can download the latest version of CMake from cmake.org. For most users that will be the Windows x64 installer file.

Once downloaded, double-click the installer file in your File Explorer to run it, and follow the on-screen instructions. Make sure to add CMake to the system PATH from the System Settings so that it is available from the command line.

Figure 2.2: System Variables editor on Windows

Installation on Linux

Use the package management system available on your flavor of Linux to install CMake.

For example using APT on Ubuntu and Debian systems:

Console

```
sudo apt update
sudo apt install cmake
```

Example 2.7: Installing CMake using apt on Debian

Fedora and RedHat Enterprise Linux systems use the Dandified YUM package manager:

Console

```
sudo dnf install cmake
```

Example 2.8: Installing CMake using yum on RedHat

In any case, once CMake is installed you make sure it works by running it from the command line:

Console

```
cmake —version
```

Example 2.9: Getting the installed version of CMake

CMake should respond with text resembling the following:

Console

```
cmake version 3.28.0

CMake suite maintained and supported by Kitware (kitware.com/
cmake).
```

Sample 2.2:Example output of the CMake program

The CMake version is useful for properly configuring the JSI compile environment on Android Studio later.

Installing Ruby

Ruby is the tool that installs Cocoapods on MacOS, a necessary component of React Native modules for iOS. You can install Ruby using the Homebrew program, like this:

Console

```
brew install ruby
```

Example 2.10: Install Ruby programming language on MacOS

Installing CocoaPods

CocoaPods is a dependency manager for Swift and ObjectiveC modules, similar to npm or yarn for JavaScript. It is written in the Ruby Language, and can be installed using the gem command provided by Ruby:

Console

```
gem install cocoapods
```

Example 2.11: Installing Cocoapod dependencies

Initialize a new React Native Project

JSI is a part of a React Native project, so any new JSI project requires first creating a React Native project. As this book gives examples in TypeScript, you may want to initialize a React Native project with TypeScript as the development language:

Console

```
npx react-native init YourProjectName \
    --template react-native-template-typescript
```

Example 2.12: Initialize a React Native project with TypeScript support

Of course you should replace "YourProjectName" with whatever project name you want to use.

If you want to program in plain JavaScript instead of TypeScript, or you want to add TypeScript support manually, you can exclude the --template parameter from the `react-native init` command:

Console

```
npx react-native init YourProjectName
```

Example 2.13:Initialize a React Native project without TypeScript support

Alternately, you may want to use Expo to power your React Native project, although JavaScript Native Interface does not yet support compiling to WebAssembly so JSI doesn't work in the browser, even though Expo supports building to Web.

Console

```
npx create-expo-app YourProjectName
```

Example 2.14: Initialize a React Native Expo App

Setting up the JSI Framework

Before Getting started writing functions, we should create our JSI library installer. This library is a C++ file that creates a name for our library, includes the JSI dependencies, and registers our library with the React Native Project.

Although you can place your Native Interface files anywhere in your project, it is customary to put these C++ files in the cpp folder of your React Native Project's root or src folder. In this example, we are creating a library called "exampleJsiLibrary":

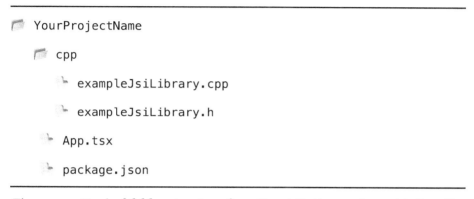

Figure 2.3: Typical folder structure for a React Native project with C++ files

In the main C++ file, we can include the common header, which we will see later.

cpp/exampleJsiLibrary.cpp

```
// include the common header for this library
#include "exampleJsiLibrary.h"
```

Example 2.15: Include std and Facebook JSI headers

Describe which namespaces we are working in so we increase the readability of our code. Two important ones so far are `facebook::jsi` and `std`. This lets is write things like `string` instead of `std::string` and `Function` instead of `facebook::jsi::Function` to make reading our code easier:

cpp/exampleJsiLibrary.cpp

```
// describe which namespaces we are using,
// so we don't have to prefix each method
// with `facebook::jsi::...`
using namespace facebook::jsi;
using namespace std;
```

Example 2.16: Set namespace for shorter function declarations

Create the installation function described in Chapter 1. In this example, we define our own namespace, `MyJsiNamespace`. This is optional but allows us use the same installer function name on multiple JSI libraries, so we are less likely to create bugs resulting from colliding function names:

cpp/exampleJsiLibrary.cpp

```cpp
// create a namespace to reference this module in code
namespace MyJsiNamespace {
  // create a function that defines your JSI functions
  void installExampleJsiLibrary(Runtime &runtime) {
    // ... define JSI functions here
    // Function functName1 = Function::createHostFunction(...);
    // runtime.global()().setProperty(...);
    // Function functName2 = Function::createHostFunction(...);
    // runtime.global()().setProperty(...);
    // ...
  }
}
```

Example 2.17:Describing the function that installs TypeScript functions

Finally we can create a header file that exposes the
`MyJsiNampespace::installExampleJsiLibrary()` function to the host
platform's language, for example Java on Android or Swift on iOS:

cpp/exampleJsiLibrary.h

```
#ifndef __MY_JSI_LIBRARY
#define __MY_JSI_LIBRARY

// include common C++ features such as string and cout
#include <iostream>
// include JSI libraries
#include <jsi/jsilib.h>
#include <jsi/jsi.h>

// allow us to use short names for JSI classes
using namespace facebook::jsi;

namespace MyJsiNampespace {
  void installExampleJsiLibrary(Runtime &runtime);
}

#endif
```

Example 2.18: Creating a sharable header file for your module

We define the same namespace and write the function definition so
calling functions can check if the parameter and return types are
correct. We wrap all that in a conditional definition so that we don't
try to define the same function multiple times if the header is included
by more than one other file.

3

Integrating Into a Project

Integrating JavaScript Native Interface into a React Native project can be a little tricky. It requires that the compiler can correctly find and build the JSI code, and that the native code (for example Swift or Java) can locate, load, and execute the resulting binary, and that the corresponding functions are correctly exposed to the React Native environment.

Any mistake in configuration or change to the version or features of one of these components can result in strange compile or runtime errors, due to compile failures, linking failures, inability to load dependent libraries or execute linked functions, memory leaks, or simply due to unexplainable application crashes such as segmentation faults or signal halts.

Even with a step-by-step tutorial, you may find unique qualities on your system that cause strange failures. It is important do document what works so that it can be reproduced and then avoid changing software versions without the ability to test or revert back to a working version.

Android

Thanks to Java, Android has long had the ability to load and run C++ code from the Java Virtual Machine. This feature is called "Java Native Interface," and it lets us run our C++ code when our Android app starts up.

Doing this of course is a little involved, as it requires configuring a C compiler, creating an interface between Java and C++, creating a few Java classes, and executing specific functions at certain times in our app lifecycle.

Let's see how to do this for Android.

Using Android Studio, open the android folder of your React Native project.

Calling the JSI Module Installer

In order to tell Java how to call the native code, we must create a bridge using the Java Native Interface which can call native code external to Java. Create a new file in your Android Studio project.

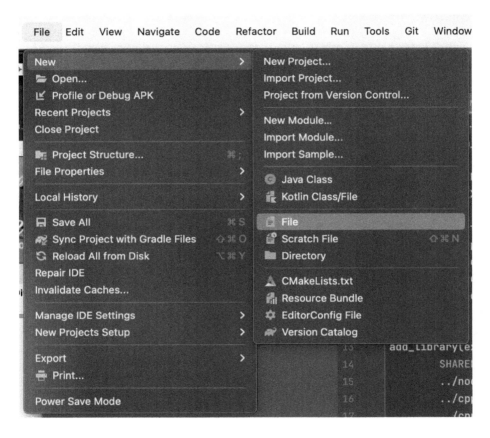

Figure 1.1: Create a new file in Android Studio

Name this file as `cpp-adapter.cpp`:

Figure 1.2: Name the new file

This file is responsible for installing the Native Interface functions by executing the `installExampleJsiLibrary()` function.

To do this, we must include the Java Native Interface (JNI) and JavaScript Native Interface headers, as well as the header for our JSI library:

C++

```
#include <jni.h>
#include <jsi/jsi.h>
#include "exampleJsiLibrary.h"
```

Sample 1.1: Include dependent libraries

To make writing code less wordy, we can declare that we are using the `facebook::jsi` namespace. This way we can write `Runtime` instead of `Facebook::jsi::Runtime` for example:

C++

```
using namespace Facebook::jsi;
```

Sample 1.2: Improve code readability by declaring namespace usage

Next we will declare that we will be running C++ code from an externally loaded library using the Java Native Interface. We will create a function that loads our library, which is named with the format `Java_<your-full-project-namespace>_initialize()`. In this example, that is `Java_com_reactnativesimplejsi_SimpleJsiModule_initialize()`. Notice the `SimpleJsiModule` in there, that class name will be important after:

C++

```
extern "C" JNIEXPORT void JNICALL
Java_com_reactnativesimplejsi_SimpleJsiModule_initialize(
  JNIEnv *env,
  jobject clazz,
  jlong jsiPtr
) {
}
```

Sample 1.3: Initialize JNI and declare expected function name

Finally we will create the code that loads our JSI module. It casts the JSI environment runtime pointer as a `Runtime` object, and then executes the `installExampleJsiLibrary()` for that runtime environment from our `exampleJsiLibrary.cpp` file.

C++

```cpp
extern "C" JNIEXPORT void JNICALL
Java_com_reactnativesimplejsi_SimpleJsiModule_initialize(...) {
    Runtime *runtime = reinterpret_cast<Runtime *>(jsiPtr);
    if (runtime) {
        MyJsiNamespace::installExampleJsiLibrary(*runtime);
    }
}
```

Sample 1.4: Install the JSI functions from our library

Putting it all together, we can see the finished JNI bridge for Android:

cpp-adapter.cpp

```cpp
#include <jni.h>
#include <jsi/jsi.h>
#include "exampleJsiLibrary.h"

using namespace facebook::jsi;

extern "C" JNIEXPORT void JNICALL
Java_com_reactnativesimplejsi_ExampleModule_initialize(
  JNIEnv *env,
  jobject clazz,
  jlong jsiPtr
) {
    Runtime *runtime = reinterpret_cast<Runtime *>(jsiPtr);
    if (runtime) {
        MyJsiNamespace::installExampleJsiLibrary(*runtime);
    }
}
```

Example 1.1: Defining Java Native Interface bridge to C++

Initialize the React Native Environment in Java

Next we need a module that can load our JSI file into memory and execute the `cpp-bridge.cpp` code to install our JSI functions.

The class must extend `ReactContextBaseJavaModule`.

Java

```
public class YourJsiModule extends ReactContextBaseJavaModule
```

Sample:

Importantly, the class must load the compiled binary from the `cpp` folder.

Java

```
public static final String myLibraryFolder = "cpp";
System.loadLibrary(myLibraryFolder);
```

Sample 1.5: Loading the JSI library using JNI

The `installExampleJsiLibrary` is the native method we wrote in the `cpp/exampleJsiLibrary.cpp` file. In Java we can declare it as a `native` method, meaning it will execute binary code rather than Java, and the `long jsi` parameter refers to the in-memory address of the loaded binary.

Java

```
public native void installExampleJsiLibrary(long jsi);
```

Sample 1.6: Defining the native function for use in Java

The ReactContextBaseJavaModule defines the public void installLib() method, where you can define how to load your library, in this case by calling the native function:

Java

```
public void installLib(JavaScriptContextHolder context) {
  this.installExampleJsiLibrary(context.get());
}
```

Sample 1.6: Calling the JSI function installer

Putting it All Together

You can put it all together by finding the SimpleJsiModule.java file in your project path.

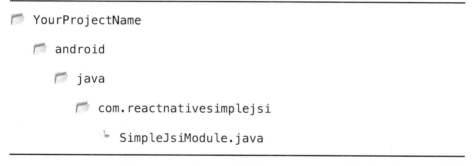

Figure 1.3: Project folder structure with SimpleJsiModule

This class extends ReactContextBaseJavaModule, loads the compiled libraries in the folder into memory, then executes the installLib method to run the installExampleJsiLibrary() from your CPP file.

SimpleJsiModule.java

```java
package com.reactnativesimplejsi;

import android.util.Log;

import androidx.annotation.NonNull;
import com.facebook.react.bridge.JavaScriptContextHolder;
import com.facebook.react.bridge.ReactApplicationContext;
import com.facebook.react.bridge.ReactContextBaseJavaModule;
import com.facebook.react.module.annotations.ReactModule;

@ReactModule(name = YourJsiModule.NAME)
public class SimpleJsiModule extends ReactContextBaseJavaModule {
  public static final String NAME = "YourProjectName";
  public static final String myLibraryFolder = "jsiExample";

  /**
   * Load the JSI binaries into memory
   */
  static {
    try {
      System.loadLibrary(myLibraryFolder);
    } catch (Exception ignored) {
    }
  }

  public YourJsiModule(ReactApplicationContext context) {
    super(context);
  }
```

Example 1.2: JSI Module

SimpleJsiModule.java (continued)

```java
  @Override
  @NonNull
  public String getName() {
    return NAME;
  }

  /**
   * Declare a Java accessor for your JSI function installer
   */
  private native void installExampleJsiLibrary(long jsi);

  /**
   * Attempt to run your JSI installer
   */
  public void installLib(JavaScriptContextHolder context) {
    if (reactContext.get() != 0) {
      this.installExampleJsiLibrary(context.get());
    } else {
      Log.e(
        this.getClass().getName(),
        "JSI Runtime is not available in debug mode"
      );
    }
  }
}
```

Example 1.3: JSI Module (continued)

Define the Package that Loads the Module

As Java development tends to favor verbosity, we must also define a Package class which is capable of creating the native modules and other relevant features.

Importantly this file extends the ReactPackage class and overrides the createNativeModules() function to load the ExampleModule when called.

Create a new file in your project called SimpleJsiModulePackage.java.

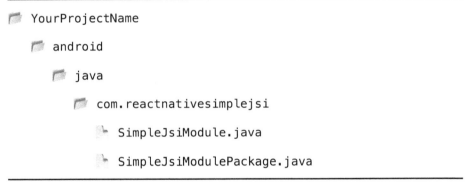

```
YourProjectName
    android
        java
            com.reactnativesimplejsi
                SimpleJsiModule.java
                SimpleJsiModulePackage.java
```

Figure 1.4: Project folder structure with Module and Package

The code for that file is as follows:

SimpleJsiModulePackage.java

```
package com.reactnativesimplejsi;
import android.util.Log;
import androidx.annotation.NonNull;
import com.facebook.react.ReactPackage;
import com.facebook.react.bridge.NativeModule;
import com.facebook.react.bridge.ReactApplicationContext;
import com.facebook.react.uimanager.ViewManager;
import java.util.Arrays;
import java.util.Collections;
import java.util.List;
public class SimpleJsiModulePackage implements ReactPackage {
    @NonNull
    @Override
    public List<NativeModule> createNativeModules(
      @NonNull ReactApplicationContext reactContext
    ) {
        Log.d("ExampleModulePackage", "createNativeModules()");
        return Arrays.<NativeModule>asList(
          new ExampleModule(reactContext)
        );
    }
    @NonNull
    @Override
    public List<ViewManager> createViewManagers(
      @NonNull ReactApplicationContext reactContext
    ) {
        Log.d("ExampleModulePackage", "createViewManagers()");
        return Collections.emptyList();
    }
}
```

Example 1.4: Module package creates native modules

Define Compiler Options

We need to tell the CMake program how the header files are related to both our project and to JavaScript Native Interface in general. This will help CMake compile and link native binaries properly.

Importantly, we must include our cpp folder and anything related to JavaScript Native Interface. Remembering that the android, cpp, and node_modules folders are all at the same level relative to the root folder, we can tell CMake to include these folders like this:

android/CMakeLists.txt

```
// ...

include_directories(
  ../cpp
  ../node_modules/react-native/React
  ../node_modules/react-native/React/Base
  ../node_modules/react-native/ReactCommon/jsi
)

// ...
```

Sample 1.8: Telling CMake which folders to when looking for headers

We also need to define our library, which we can call exampleJsiLibrary. This will expose the header for other parts of the program to verify the declared functions.

android/CMakeLists.txt

```
// ...

add_library(exampleJsiLibrary
  SHARED
  ../node_modules/react-native/ReactCommon/jsi/jsi/jsi.cpp
  ../cpp/exampleJsiLibrary.cpp
  ../cpp/exampleJsiLibrary.h
)

// ...
```

Sample 1.9: Telling CMake that our code is runnable by other programs

Finally, we want to set our library as linkable to other parts of our program, using the `target_link_libraries()` function. The name `exampleJsiLibrary` in this context defines the name of the output file, which must be the same as what we tell Java in the previous step.

android/CMakeLists.txt

```
target_link_libraries(exampleJsiLibrary)
```

Sample 1.10: Make our library linkable to other programs

The final `CMakeLists.txt` looks like this. Recall the version of CMake you installed earlier to set the version:

android/CMakeLists.txt

```
cmake_minimum_required(VERSION 3.28.0)

set (CMAKE_VERBOSE_MAKEFILE ON)
set (CMAKE_CXX_STANDARD 11)

include_directories(
  ../cpp
  ../node_modules/react-native/React
  ../node_modules/react-native/React/Base
  ../node_modules/react-native/ReactCommon/jsi
)

add_library(exampleJsiLibrary
  SHARED
  ../node_modules/react-native/ReactCommon/jsi/jsi/jsi.cpp
  ../cpp/exampleJsiLibrary.cpp
  ../cpp/exampleJsiLibrary.h
)
target_link_libraries(sequel)
```

Example 1.5: CMake instructions

Tell Gradle to Compile JSI Module

Open the example/android in Android Studio and wait for Gradle to build your project. After, you should see the following folder structure in your side bar.

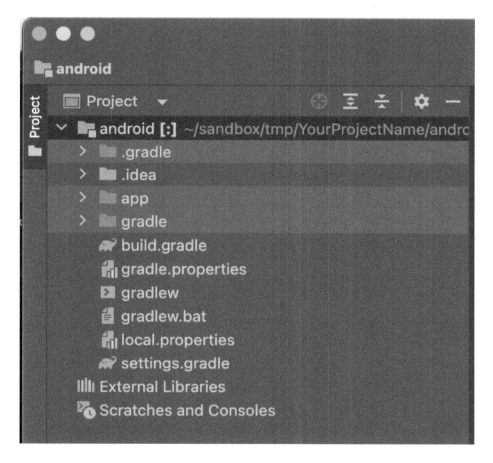

Figure 1.6: Android Studio project folder

Open your bundle.gradle file from your app module and add a section
under android called externalNativeBuild which includes
information about which CMake version and instructions are used to
compile the native library.

build.gradle

```
android {android {
  ...
  externalNativeBuild {
    cmake {
      path "./CMakeLists.txt"
      version "3.28.0+"
    }
  }
}
```

Sample 1.11: Gradle configuration for CMAke

With these changes, you should have a complete compile chain that
builds your JSI module and your Android app, plus the Java code to
load it as a JNI into memory and the bridge to call the installer
function to attach the JSI functions to the JavaScript global context.

iOS

On iOS, the bridge is handled using Objective C. To make sure you have the right dependencies installed for iOS, you must install the CocoaPod dependencies for your React Native project using the `pod` command:

Console

```
cd ios
pod install
cd ..
```

Sample 1.12: Installing CocoaPods dependencies for React Native project

Once the dependencies are installed, you can start writing code. Open the Xcode Workspace file to work with your project in Xcode. You can do that by opening `YourProjectName.xcworkspace` from your file manager or by opening it from the Terminal:

Console

```
open ios/YourProjectName.xcworkspace &
```

Sample 1.13: Open Xcode project from Terminal

Link C++ Files to Xcode Project

Xcode doesn't store source code in the same way as a normal code editor, so it's important to link the C++ files into the project before working with them. Do this by dragging and dropping the cpp folder from your Finder into the root of your project folder on Xcode.

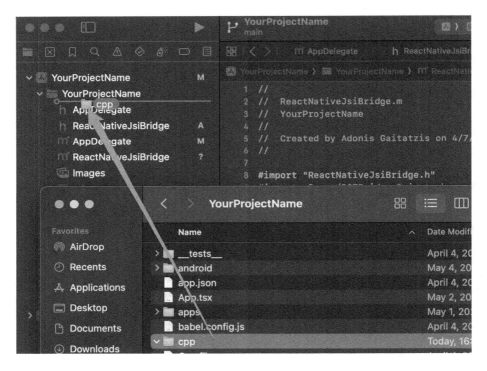

Figure 1.7: Dragging the cpp folder into the Xcode project

After dropping, Xcode will ask if the files should be copied. Make sure to unselect "Copy items if needed" as enabling this option can result in you working on your C++ files from another editor without realizing that the Xcode version of those files have never changed.

Select the option to "Create groups" to preserve the `cpp` folder structure in your project:

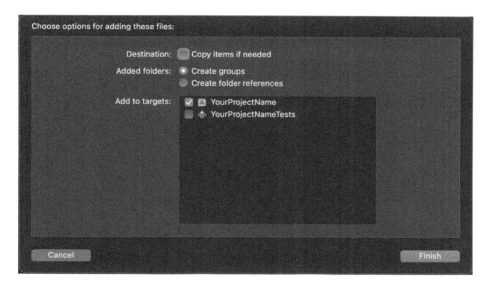

Figure 1.8: Linking cpp folder to Xcode project

Call JSI Installer Function from Objective C

In the main menu, open the "File" menu and select "New" -> "File" to reveal the new file dialog. Select an Objective-C file in the modal dialog:

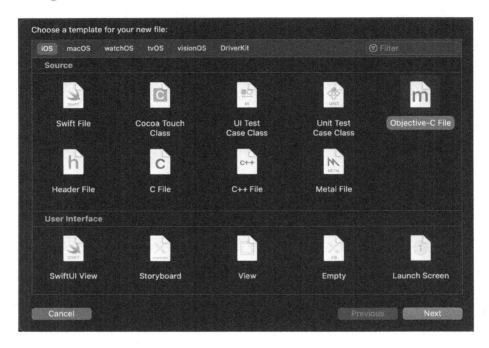

Figure 1.9: Creating an Objective-C file

Name the file. In this example we will call it `ReactNativeJsiBridge.mm`, as it's job is to create a bridge between the React Native runtime and the JSI module installer.

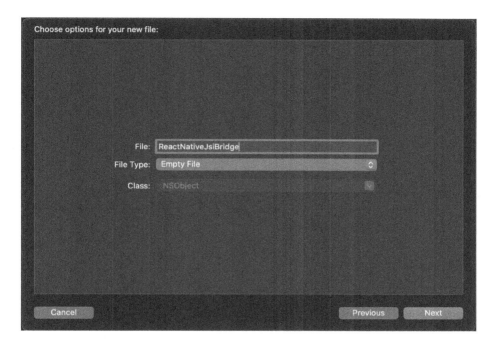

Figure 1.10: Naming an Objective-C File

Create another file, this time a Header file called `ReactNativeJsiBridge.h`.

Open the new `ReactNativeJsiBridge.mm` file so we can write Objective-C code that loads the JSI module into memory and executes its `installExampleJsiLibrary()` function.

Importantly, this file will import the header file associated with your JSI library. Notice that, because we have linked the cpp folder into our project, we can reference it as if it's in the same folder as the Objective-C code.

ios/ReactNativeJsiBridge.h

```
#import "cpp/exampleJsiLibrary.h"
```

Sample 1.14: Including the JSI code

It must also include libraries necessary for interacting with React Native and JSI:

ios/ReactNativeJsiBridge.h

```
#import "ReactNativeJsiBridge.h"
#import <React/RCTBridge+Private.h>
#import <React/RCTUtils.h>
#import <jsi/jsi.h>
```

Sample 1.15: Including the React Native bridge and JSI dependencies

The code creates a new module that interacts with the React Native Bridge, called YourJsiModule:

ios/ReactNativeJsiBridge.mm

```
@implementation ReactNativeJsiBridge

RCT_EXPORT_MODULE()

// @synthesize methodQueue = _methodQueue;
// ...
// @synthesize bridge = _bridge;
// ...

@end
```

Sample 1.16: Defining the exported module through the React Native Bridge

It will run code on the main thread, or "queue" as its called in Objective-C:

ios/ReactNativeJsiBridge.mm

```
@synthesize methodQueue = _methodQueue;
+ (BOOL)requiresMainQueueSetup {
    return YES;
}
```

Sample 1.17:Declaring that code runs on main thread by default

It will use the React Native Bridge to interact between native code and JavaScript, to run the `installExampleJsiLibrary` method from our JSI file. In this example, the installer function is in the `MyJsiNamespace` namespace:

ios/ReactNativeJsiBridge.mm

```
@synthesize bridge = _bridge;

- (void)setBridge:(RCTBridge *)bridge {
    _bridge = bridge;
    _setBridgeOnMainQueue = RCTIsMainQueue();
    RCTCxxBridge *cxxBridge = (RCTCxxBridge *)self.bridge;
    if (cxxBridge.runtime) {
        MyJsiNamespace::installExampleJsiLibrary(
            *(facebook::jsi::Runtime *)cxxBridge.runtime
        );
    }
}
```

Sample 1.18: Connecting JSI to React Native Bridge and installing functions

If you chose not to define a namespace for your JSI installer function, you can simply call it without namespace prefix, like this:

C++

```
installExampleJsiLibrary(
    *(facebook::jsi::Runtime *)cxxBridge.runtime
);
```

Sample 1.19: Calling JSI installer function without a namespace prefix

Putting it All Together

You can put it all together by finding the ReactNativeJsiBridge.h and ReactNativeJsiBridge.mm files in your project path in Xcode, as well as the cpp folder you linked.

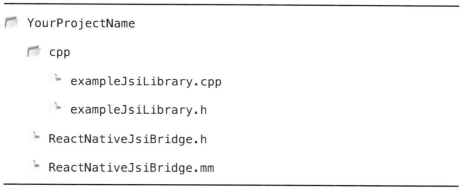

Figure 1.11: React Native Bridge file structure in Xcode

The ReactNativeJsiBridge.mm file contains the following code, described already:

ios/ReactNativeJsiBridge.mm

```
#import "ReactNativeJsiBridge.h"

@implementation ReactNativeJsiBridge

@synthesize bridge = _bridge;
@synthesize methodQueue = _methodQueue;

RCT_EXPORT_MODULE()

+ (BOOL)requiresMainQueueSetup {
    return YES;
}

- (void)setBridge:(RCTBridge *)bridge {
    _bridge = bridge;
    _setBridgeOnMainQueue = RCTIsMainQueue();
    RCTCxxBridge *cxxBridge = (RCTCxxBridge *)self.bridge;
    if (cxxBridge.runtime) {
        MyJsiNamespace::installExampleJsiLibrary(
            *(facebook::jsi::Runtime *)cxxBridge.runtime
        );
    }
}

@end
```

Example 1.6: Describing the React Native Bridge to the Native Interface

The ReactNativeJsiBridge.h file imports and extends the RCTBridgeModule.h class to link features related to loading and running your native binary through the React Native Bridge.

ReactNativeJsiBridge.h

```
#ifndef ReactNativeJsiBridge_h
#define ReactNativeJsiBridge_h

#import <React/RCTBridge+Private.h>
#import <React/RCTBridgeModule.h>
#import <React/RCTUtils.h>
#import <jsi/jsi.h>
#import "cpp/exampleJsiLibrary.h"

@interface ReactNativeJsiBridge : NSObject <RCTBridgeModule>;
@property (nonatomic, assign) BOOL setBridgeOnMainQueue;
@end

#endif
```

Example 1.7: Exposing the setBridgeOnMainQueue through header

That's all for iOS. When you compile your project for iOS Simulator or a device, the ReactNativeJsiBridge object will automatically be compiled and your project will load.

Calling JSI Methods in TypeScript

By default, TypeScript has a pre-defined understanding of what functions and variables are included in the global object. For example, functions such as parseInt() and atob() are part of the default JavaScript global context.

Therefore, you can call parseInt() directly, which is the same as calling global.parseInt().

JavaScript Native Interface functions are not part of the default global object definition, meaning that your editor and the TypeScript compiler will throw errors when you try to call a JSI function in your TypeScript code, for example if we try to call a JSI method called yourJsiFunctionName() from React Native:

App.tsx

```
const onPress = () => {
  yourJsiFunctionName();
}
```

Sample 1.19: Calling an un-typed JSI function in TypeScript

Your editor should underline the yourJsiFunctionName() function as it doesn't exist in the known global context. When you run your React Native, the console will print a message like this when you try to execute the yourJsiFunctionName() function:

Console

```
ReferenceError: Property 'yourJsiFunctionName' doesn't exist,
js engine: hermes
```

Sample 1.20: TypeError thrown when calling an unknown JSI function

To let TypeScript know that a JSI function exists, we can define it by writing its method signature in a declare block, like this:

App.tsx

```
declare global {
  yourJsiFunctionName(param: type): type;
}
```

Sample 1.21: Declaring JSI functions in the global context

After, the editor will no longer complain about the new function and the JavaScript engine will execute the function.

4

Function 1: Accepts No Parameters and Returns Void

In your React Native code, you may want to execute a function that performs some action but doesn't return a value. In TypeScript, we tend to define such a function like this:

Resulting TypeScript Function Definition

```
const functionName = () => void;
```

Sample 4.1: Function with no parameters and returns void

> *Note: In JSI, we aim to create a function that TypeScript sees the way we've written in such a function declaration, even though the JSI is written in C++. In this book we will often use the TypeScript function declaration to demonstrate how a JSI behaves in the world of TypeScript. We do this because it allows us to understand the outcome of the C++ declaration from the perspective of the language we will be calling the method from.*

A common example of such a function in React Native is the button onPress() function, which is often implemented like this:

TypeScript

```
const onPress = () => {
  console.log("button clicked");
};
```

Sample 4.2: Button onPress() function logs to the console

For example, let's say we have a JSI function called simplePrint() which writes Hello World to the console.

TypeScript Call

If we call such a function from an onPress() method inside React Native, the implementation would look like this:

TypeScript

```
const onPress = () => {
    simplePrint();
}
```

Sample 4.3: Calling the simplePrint() function on button press handler

JSI Implementation

The corresponding JSI function won't take any parameters or return a value. Instead it could use `std::cout` to echo text to the console, for example:

C++

```
cout << "Hello World " << endl;
```

Sample 4.4: Echoing "Hello World" to the console

> *Note: It is possible that `cout` or `println()` will not print to the same console as the React Native terminal. It may instead log to a different terminal such as the Android logger, the Xcode log, or somewhere else entirely.*

Inside the `installExampleJsiLibrary` function, we must create and register a new function using the `jsi::createFunctionFromHost` function, which accepts certain parameters including:

- The React Native runtime context,

- The desired name of the function, in this example, "simplePrint",

- The number of parameters the function will accept (in this case 0),

- The lambda function that actually executes the resulting function, which takes:

  - The runtime context,

  - The parameter list, and

  - The number of parameters

The lambda function returns a data type called a
facebook::jsi::Value, compatible with JavaScript's generic data
types.

> Note: Recall that C++ arrays are just a pointer to a memory
> address and don't contain knowledge about how many items are in
> the array, so it is important to know the array length as a separate
> value.

In JavaScript, an undefined return value is implicit in any function
that doesn't explicitly return data. So this function which doesn't
explicitly return a value:

TypeScript

```
const exampleFunction = () => {
    // do something
}
```

Sample 4.5: Implicitly return undefined

Is the same as this function which explicitly returns undefined:

TypeScript

```
const exampleFunction = (): void => {
    // do something
    return undefined;
}
```

Sample 4.5: Explicitly return undefined

In C++, the lambda requires a Value to be returned, we must return some Value-compatible data, even if it is undefined. Later chapters will show how to return other data types, but for now we will return undefined like by calling the Value::undefined() static method:

C++

```
HostFunctionType lambda = [](...) -> Value {
  // do something
  return Value::undefined();
}
```

Sample 4.6: Return an undefined Value in JSI

We declare a new JavaScript Native Interface function named simplePrint() like this:

C++

```
Function simplePrintFunc = Function::createFromHostFunction(
  runtime,
  PropNameID::forAscii(runtime, "simplePrint"),
  0, // <- zero parameters
  [](
    Runtime &runtime,
    const Value &thisValue,
    const Value *arguments,
    size_t count
  ) -> Value {
    // execute code here
    cout << "Hello World" << endl;
  }
);
```

Sample 4.7: Create a JSI function with no parameters:

Unlike TypeScript, we must always explicitly return a value in C++. Since the `simplePrint()` function implicitly return `void` or `undefined`, we will explicitly create one using the `facebook::jsi::Value::undefined()` static method and return that in our C++ code.

C++

```
Function simplePrintFunc = Function::createFromHostFunction(
  ...
  [](...) -> Value {
    cout << "Hello World" << endl;
    return Value::undefined();
  }
);
```

Sample 4.8: Returning an empty value

Lastly we register this JSI function to be callable from within React Native, so that JavaScript can know that the function name `simplePrint` refers to the `simplePrintFunction` JSI function. We do this by using the `Global.setProperty()` method to link the name `simplePrint` in the React Native runtime environment to the pointer to the `jsi::Function` we just created.

C++

```
runtime.global().setProperty(
  runtime,
  "simplePrint",
  simplePrintFunc
);
```

Sample 4.9: Make the the JSI function callable from JavaScript

Since the PropNameId and the global property should have the same name, we can simplify the code a little by calling the .utf8() method to retrieve the PropNameId as a UTF-8 std::string, like this:

C++

```cpp
PropNameId simplePrintName = PropNameID::forAscii(
  runtime,
  "simplePrint"
);
Function simplePrintFunc = Function::createFromHostFunction(
  runtime,
  simplePrintName,
  // ...
);
runtime.global().setProperty(
  runtime,
  simplePrintName.utf8(),
  simplePrintFunc
);
```

Sample 4.10: Separating the PropNameId to increase code reusability

Note: Knowing that the lambda function is a facebook::jsi::HostFunctionType type, we can choose to separate the lambda from the JSI function declaration, like this:

C++

```
// Property name
PropNameId simplePrintPropId = PropNameID::forAscii(
  runtime,
  "simplePrint"
);


// Define the lambda
HostFunctionType simplePrintLambda = [](
    Runtime &runtime,
    const Value &thisValue,
    const Value *arguments,
    size_t count
) -> Value {
    // echo to the console
    cout << "Hello from C++" << endl;
    // return a TypeScript-compatible undefined value
    return Value::undefined();
}


// Create the host function
Function simplePrintFunc = Function::createFromHostFunction(
  runtime,
  simplePrintPropId,
  0,
  simplePrintLambda
);
```

Sample 4.11: Separating lambda and property name from JSI declaration

Putting it All Together

We can put these concepts together into a single function call that registers a JSI function which executes a lambda that echoes "Hello World" to the console and returns an undefined-compatible `Value`:

cpp/exampleJsiLibrary.cpp

```cpp
// ... includes and namespace
void installExampleJsiLibrary(Runtime &runtime) {
  PropNameId simplePrintName = PropNameID::forAscii(
    runtime,
    "simplePrint"
  );
  Function simplePrintFunc = Function::createFromHostFunction(
    runtime,
    PropNameID::forAscii(runtime, "simplePrint"),
    0,
    [](
      Runtime &runtime,
      const Value &thisValue,
      const Value *arguments,
      size_t count
    ) -> Value
    {
      // echo to the console
      cout << "Hello from C++" << endl;
      // return a TypeScript-compatible undefined value
      return Value::undefined();
    }
  );
  runtime.global().setProperty(
    runtime,
    simplePrintName.utf8(),
    simplePrintFunc
  );
}
```

Example 4.6: Install and link a JSI Function using C++

Be sure to declare the function in your global context to make the TypeScript compiler and your editor aware that this function is available:

TypeScript

```
declare global {
  function simplePrint(): void;
}
```

Sample 4.12: Declaring a JSI function in TypeScript

5

Function 2: Accepts No Parameters and Returns a String

Many times it is useful for a function to return a value. This is especially true on React Native where the user can't see what is printed in the console.

For this reason, we want to make a function that returns some data, for example a JavaScript `string` containing the text "Hello World".

In Typescript, we tend to define such a function like this:

Resulting TypeScript Function Definition

```
const functionName = () => string;
```

Sample 5.1: Function with no parameters and returns a string

Let's say we call such a function from an `onPress()` method inside React Native, setting a variable to the returned value. The implementation would look like this:

TypeScript

```
const onPress = () => {
  const stringValue: string = returnString();
  console.log(stringValue); // "Hello World"
}
```

Sample 5.2: Calling a method that returns a string from a Button press

JSI Implementation

The corresponding JSI function is declared the same as the previous example, including the `Value` return.

The difference is that instead of returning a `Value::undefined()`, the lambda function returns `Value` containing a `facebook::jsi::String` object.

> *Note: the `facebook::jsi::String` type is different from the `std::string` type you may already be familiar with in C++. `String` is specifically designed to be JavaScript-compatible and supports UTF-8 character encoding.*

There are two methods for creating `String`s in JSI:

Static Method	Explanation
`createFromUtf8`	Create a UTF-8 compatible JavaScript `String`
`createFromAscii`	Create an ASCII compatible JavaScript `String`

Table 5.1: String creation methods in JavaScript Native Interface

To create a UTF-8 compatible `String`, simply pass text into the static `createFromUtf8` method:

C++

```
String s = String::createFromUtf8(runtime, "Hello World");
```

Sample 5.3: Create a UTf-8 compatible String in JSI

To create an ASCII-compatible String, use the createFromAscii() static method instead:

C++

```
String s = String::createFromAscii(runtime, "Hello World");
```

Sample 5.4: Create an ASCII compatible String in JSI

> *Note: A good rule of thumb is that if you are working with human-language text, you should always use UTF-8 as it supports accented characters foreign language characters, and other symbols. If you are using String objects to serialize large binary data such as encryption keys or image data, you should use ASCII since it cooperates with large binary data well.*

JSI supports returning a Value return type, not a String, so it is important to wrap the String into a Value object when returning a string in a JSI function. To do this, you must create and return a Value object from the String, like this:

C++

```
return Value(runtime, s);
```

Sample 5.5: Return a String as a JavaScript-compatible Value

Putting it All Together

We can put these concepts together into a single function call that registers a JSI function which executes a lambda that returns "Hello World" from a string-like, JavaScript-compatible Value object:

cpp/exampleJsiLibrary.cpp

```
void installExampleJsiLibrary(Runtime &runtime) {
  // create a function the same way
  Function returnStringFunc = Function::createFromHostFunction(
    runtime,
    PropNameID::forAscii(runtime, "returnString"),
    0,
    [](
      Runtime &runtime,
      const Value &thisValue,
      const Value *arguments,
      size_t count
    ) -> Value {
      // return a Value that represents a string
      return Value(
        runtime,
        // create a string from UTF-8 text
        String::createFromUtf8(runtime, "Hello World")
      );
    }
  );

  // register the function as callable
  runtime.global().setProperty(
    runtime,
    "returnString",
    returnStringFunc
  );
}
```

Example 5.1: A JSI function that returns the string "Hello World"

Don't forget to declare the function in your global context to make the TypeScript compiler and your editor aware that this function is available:

TypeScript

```typescript
declare global {
    function returnString(): string;
}
```

Sample 4.6: Declaring a JSI function in TypeScript

6

Function 3: Returns Primitive Type

Strings aren't the only thing a function can return. Sometimes you want to return types other than string from your JSI code, for example number, null, or undefined.

For example a function that returns a number, such as a random number generator:

Example TypeScript Function Definition

```
const getRandomNumber = () => number;
```

Sample 6.1: Function with no parameters and returns a number

Such a function can be called from TypeScript like this:

TypeScript

```
const onPress = () => {
  const numberValue: number = getRandomNumber();
  console.log(numberValue); // 37
}
```

Sample 6.2: Calling a random number generator from a Button press

It is even possible have a function that returns one of several types, although it's generally not a good practice to implement such methods as it makes type checking difficult.

Example TypeScript Function Definition

```
const exampleFunc = () => string |
  number |
  boolean |
  null |
  undefined;
```

Sample 6.3: Function with no parameters, returns any primitive data type

Returns Primitive Type

Such a function can be called from TypeScript like this. In this example, each time `exampleFunc()` is called it returns a different value:

TypeScript

```
const onPress = () => {
  const value1 = exampleFunc();
  console.log(typeof val1, val1); // string Hello World

  const value2 = exampleFunc();
  console.log(typeof value2, value2); // boolean true

  const value3 = exampleFunc();
  console.log(typeof value3, value3); // number 37

  const value4 = exampleFunc();
  console.log(typeof value4, value4); // object null

  const value5 = exampleFunc();
  console.log(typeof value5, value5); // undefined undefined
}
```

Sample 6.4: Function returns random-typed result

A common way this pattern is implemented in TypeScript is to have a function that returns a data or either `undefined` or `null` depending on the circumstance, so that it is easy to check the type after to know if meaningful data was returned:

Function returning a value or undefined

```
const exampleFunction = () => number | undefined;
```

Sample 6.5: Function returns number under some circumstances

Say for example we are looking up a user's email address on a system where, if the user is logged in the email address will be returned and if the user is not logged in, the function will return undefined:

TypeScript

```
const onPress = () => {
    const userEmail: string | undefined = getUserEmail();
    if (userEmail === undefined) {
      console.log("User not logged in");
    } else {
      console.log(userEmail); // "email@example.com"
    }
}
```

Sample 6.6: Determine login state of user by checking if email is undefined

JSI Implementation

All of these primitive types are returned as facebook::jsi::Value objects though JSI back to React Native:

Return a number

By passing any double value into the Value constructor, it will be converted to a JavaScript-compatible number type. For example, here is how to return the number 37.5 back to JavaScript:

C++

```
Value numberValue = Value(37.5);
```

Sample 6.7: Create a JSI number Value

Since the lambda function returns a `Value`, the JSI implementation simply needs to return the number as a Value:

C++

```cpp
void exampleJsiLibrary(Runtime &runtime) {
  // number
  Function returnNum = Function::createFromHostFunction(..., {
    return Value(37.5);
  });
  runtime.global().setProperty(...);
}
```

Sample 6.8: Returning a numeric Value in JSI

Since JavaScript automatically reduces the number of significant figures of `number` types, passing `return Value(37.0000);` in JSI will automatically convert to a `37` in JavaScript and TypeScript.

Return a boolean

To create a `boolean` value, simply pass a `true` or `false` into the `Value` constructor. Here is how to create true in JSI:

C++

```cpp
Value trueValue = Value(true);
```

Sample 6.9: Create a JSI boolean Value

Creating a `false` value is similar to `true`:

C++

```cpp
Value falseValue = Value(false);
```

Sample 6.10: Create a JSI boolean Value

Just as with a `number`, we can return the `boolean` directly from a JSI lambda function:

C++

```cpp
void exampleJsiLibrary(Runtime &runtime) {
  Function getTrue = Function::createFromHostFunction(..., {
    return Value(true);
  });
  runtime.global().setProperty(...);
}
```

Sample 6.11: Return a boolean value in JSI

Return null

Creating a `null` value is even easier. Just instantiate an empty `Value` object:

C++

```cpp
Value nullValue = Value();
```

Sample 6.12: Create a JSI null Value

Just as with a string and number, null is returned as a Value through the JSI lambda function:

C++

```
void exampleJsiLibrary(Runtime &runtime) {
  Function getNull = Function::createFromHostFunction(..., {
    return Value();
  });
  runtime.global().setProperty(...);
}
```

Sample 6.13: Return a null value from a JSI function

Return undefined

To create undefined in JSI, you here can call the undefined() static method from Value:

C++

```
Value undefinedValue = Value::undefined();
```

Sample 6.14: Create a JSI undefined Value

Since Value::undefined() returns a Value type, you can simply return it through the JSI lambda function to return undefined to React Native:

C++

```cpp
void exampleJsiLibrary(Runtime &runtime) {
    Function getUndefined = Function::createFromHostFunction(...{
        return Value::undefined();
    });
    runtime.global().setProperty(...);
}
```

Sample 6.15: Return an undefined value in a JSI function

Return number or undefined

Since all return types are Value objects in JSI, you can return a number Value or an undefined Value (or String or null or any other) from the lambda function.

The example described at the beginning of the chapter is a function that returns either a number or undefined. We can implement a function like this, for example returning the number 37 or undefined depending on the outcome of a random number generator:

C++

```
#include <iostream>
#include <random>

void exampleJsiLibrary(Runtime &runtime) {
  // number
  Function numOrUndef = Function::createFromHostFunction(..., {
    random_device rd;   // Get random number from hardware
    mt19937 gen(rd()); // Seed the generator
    uniform_int_distribution<> distrib(0, 1); // set range
    int randomNumber = distrib(gen); // random [0..1]
    if (randomNumber % 2 == 0) {
      return Value::undefined();
    } else {
      return Value(37);
    }
  });
  runtime.global().setProperty(...);
}
```

Sample 6.16: Randomly return a number or undefined in a JSI function

As always, this function can't be used properly until it is declared in the global context in TypeScript:

TypeScript

```
declare global {
    function exampleFunction(): number | undefined;
}
```

Sample 6.16: Declaring a JSI function in TypeScript

7

Function 4: Accepts Primitive Type Parameters

In addition to returning values, it is important to be able to shape a function's execution by passing parameters into it. These values, sometimes also called *arguments* are what a function acts on to return some result.

In TypeScript, these parameters are typed, meaning that we can expect that each parameter is of type `string`, `number`, `object`, `null`, `undefined` or some combination of those.

For example a function that takes a single `string` parameter called name and returns "Hello " + `name` would be defined like this:

Resulting TypeScript Function Definition

```
const exampleFunction = (name: string) => string;
```

Sample 7.1: Function with one string parameter and returns a string

Another example is a function that takes two numbers and adds them together, returning the result would be defined like this:

Resulting TypeScript Function Definition

```
const exampleFunction = (
  number1: number,
  number2: number
) => number;
```

Sample 7.2: Function with two number parameter and returns a number

TypeScript functions can accept multiple types for any parameter, for example this function that converts any of true, false, "true", "false", 1, 0, null, or undefined to to a boolean version of that value:

Resulting TypeScript Function Definition

```
const toBoolean = (
  input: string | number | boolean | null | undefined
) => boolean;
```

Sample 7.3: Function accepts multiple types for parameter, returns boolean

TypeScript can also accept arrays and an any type:

Resulting TypeScript Function Definition

```
const exampleFunction = (parameter: any) => void;
```

Sample 7.4: Function accepts any type for parameter

Additionally, TypeScript supports sending optional parameters to a function. TypeScript generally treats these values as undefined.

For example:

Resulting TypeScript Function Definition

```
const exampleFunction = (
  mandatoryParameter: string,
  optionalParameter?: string
) => void;
```

Sample 7.5: Function accepts an optional parameter

Let's take for example a function which converts any string, number, boolean, null, or undefined to a boolean. For example it attempts to turn "true" and 1 into true, and "false" and 0 into false. Such a function might look like this:

Resulting TypeScript Function Definition

```
const toBoolean = (
  input: string | number | boolean | null | undefined
) => boolean;
```

Sample 7.6: Function converts any type into a boolean

Using such a function, it is possible to send one of several types as a parameter and for the function to accept the parameters and execute the function properly.

TypeScript

```
const onPress = () => {
  // string true
  console.log("string", toBoolean("true"));
  // number true
  console.log("number", toBoolean(1));
  // boolean true
  console.log("boolean", toBoolean(true));

  // string false
  console.log("string", toBoolean("false"));
  // number false
  console.log("number", toBoolean(0));
  // boolean false
  console.log("boolean", toBoolean(false));
  // null false
  console.log("null", toBoolean(null));
  // undefined false
  console.log("undefined", toBoolean(undefined));
}
```

Sample 7.7: Sending multiple types to function parameter

Let's see how to implement a function with parameters having multiple types in JSI.

JSI Implementation

The `Function::createFromHostFunction()` takes a parameter called `unsigned int paramCount` which specifies the number of parameters being sent into the function. This is necessary since the next parameter, `HostFunctionType func` contains a `Value*` parameter representing the pointer to an an array of inbound arguments.

At this point it is important to distinguish between the word "parameter" and "argument." In this book, a "parameter" is the defined data types that can be passed into a function, and an "argument" is what data that is passed into the function during runtime.

For example, parameter:

TypeScript

```
const exampleFunction = (parameter: string) => void;
```

Sample 7.8: Defining a function parameter

Compare that to an argument:

TypeScript

```
const argument = "Hello World";
exampleFunction(argument);
```

Sample 7.9: Passing an argument to a function

In the next chapter, we will see how to process multiple arguments, but for now it is important to know that the `paramCount` argument of the `createFromHostFunction()` method must match the number of expected function parameters. For example the following TypeScript function takes one parameter:

TypeScript

```
const exampleFunction = (param: string) => void;
```

Sample 7.10: TypeScript function with one parameter

The corresponding JSI function must declare a single parameter:

C++

```
Function exampleFunction = Function::createFromHostFunction(
  runtime,
  PropNameID::forAscii(runtime, "exampleFunction"),
  1,
  exampleFunctionDefinition
);
```

Sample 7.11: JSI function with one parameter

In the lambda function, the arguments can be accessed from the arguments array, like this:

C++

```cpp
HostFunctionType exampleFunctionDefinition = [](
    Runtime &runtime,
    const Value &thisValue,
    const Value *arguments,
    size_t count
) -> Value {
    // get the first argument
    const Value &argument = arguments[0];
    return Value::undefined();
}
```

Sample 7.12: Extracting a single argument from the lambda arguments

JavaScript doesn't do strict type checking. Under the hood, a string is interchangeable with a number for example. C++ on the other hand has very strict types, meaning that sending a number in place of a string will result in an error.

In TypeScript, this sort of type checking is checked but not actually enforced by the runtime environment. This means that JSI allows any data type to be sent as a generic Value to a function. Since C++ works on use strict types such as string, bool, or double, it is necessary to convert between JavaScript's generic data type and the strict types in C++. The facebook::jsi::Value object provides methods to check and convert the type represented by the JavaScript data into C++ primitives.

The first step is to check what data type the argument is, then to convert it to the appropriate native C++ type before working on it.

Determine Argument Type

As the Value object has functions to test what data primitive it contains, it is possible to go check if the Value represents one or more expected TypeScript types.

Test for String

For example, to determine if an argument is a string, check if it returns true to .toString():

C++

```
Function exampleFunc = Function::createFromHostFunction(... {
    // get argument as a reference to a facebook::jsi::Value
    const Value &argument = arguments[0];
    // true if the argument is a `string`
    bool isString = argument.isString();
});
```

Sample 7.13: Check if an argument is a string type

Test for Number

To test if an argument is a number, see if .isNumber() returns true

C++

```
bool isNumber = argument.isNumber();
```

Sample 7.14: Check if an argument is a number type

Test for Null

An argument will return `true` to `.isNull()` if it is `null`

C++

```
bool isNull = argument.isNull();
```

Sample 7.15: Check if an argument is a `null` value

Test for Undefined

To test if an argument is `undefined`, see if `.isUndefined()` returns `true`.

C++

```
bool isUndefined = argument.isUndefined();
```

Sample 7.16: Check if an argument is an `undefined` value

JavaScript and JSI support other, more complex data types such as objects, functions, and arrays which will be described later in this book.

Converting Parameters to Native Types

The `facebook::jsi::Value` object is a sort of generic type container that is not compatible with primitive types in native C++.

In JSI there are two types of conversion to native types, *get-* and *as-*. In general, attempting to *get-* an incorrect type will result in a program crash. For this reason the following code must be tested and an error thrown manually:

C++

```
bool isNumber = argument.isNumber();
if (!isNull) {
  throw JSError(runtime, "Invalid type: expected a number");
}
double number = argument.getNumber();
```

Sample 7.17: Checking if an argument is correct type before conversion

However if we convert to a value using *as-*, we will get a warning in the React Native console and the app will continue running but the function will abort and a warning will be raised. Using this method to convert the Value to a native type, like this:

C++

```
Double number = argument.asNumber();
```

Sample 7.18: Convert argument using asNumber()

Using this method will result in the following error:

Console

```
Possible unhandled Promise rejection (id: 0): Error: Exception
in HostFunction: Value is a string, expected a number
```

Sample 7.19: Type conversion error

For this reason it is always preferable to check the incoming argument types and throw errors so that the app doesn't crash unexpectedly and TypeScript developer has access to good debugging information.

In this book, we prefer the *get-* method of type conversion.

To work with primitive types such as double or string, you must convert the Value to a native type using a method provided in the Value object, based on the type of data it contains.

Convert to bool

It is possible to convert JavaScript Values into bool values with a simple call to .getBool() method.

C++

```
bool b = getBool();
```

Sample 7.20: Convert argument to a C++ bool

Convert to std::string

It is possible to convert JavaScript Values into std::string values.

JavaScript works with UTF-8 character encoding by default, making it safe to use with accent characters and non-latin glyphs such as Cyrillic, Chinese, Arabic, and Ethiopian scripts.

To convert JavaScript strings to std::strings, use the String.utf8() function on the argument:

C++

```
string s = argument.getString(runtime).utf8(runtime);
```

Sample 7.21: Convert argument to a C++ string

If your string represents ASCII data such as hex codes and encryption keys, you then you can use the same .utf8() method without worrying about character encoding issues.

Convert to `double`

The `Value` type has the ability to export to a native double-precision floating-point number using the `.getNumber()` function.

C++

```
double d = argument.getNumber();
```

Sample 7.22: Convert argument to a native double

Convert to `int`

JavaScript doesn't have a concept of `int` or `float` the way that C++ does. Instead it has only one number type. This means that a number can only be converted directly to a double in native code, since there's no way for JavaScript to know the precision of the number.

However, once the number is a `double` in our native code, we can use standard C++ functions to cast to any other number format, for example `int`:

C++

```
int i = static_cast<int>(argument.getNumber());
```

Sample 7.23: Convert argument to a native int

Convert to `NULL`

There is no `.getNull()` in Javascript Native Interface. Instead, since we can check if a `Value` is `NULL` using `.isNull()`, we can simply assign a variable to `NULL` when `.isNull()` is `true`, like this:

C++

```
string exampleParam;
if (argument.isNull()) {
  exampleParam = NULL;
}
```

Sample 7.24: Set a variable to null when the Value is null

As C++ doesn't support an undefined type, there may be times where you want to use NULL in the native code in place of JavaScript's undefined type, like this:

C++

```
string exampleParam;
if (argument.isUndefined()) {
  exampleParam = NULL;
}
```

Sample 7.25: Set a variable to null when the Value is undefined

Type Conversion Errors

It is recommended necessary to check the Value type before attempting a conversion to a native type, because JSI handles type conversion errors by crashing the app or aborting the function. Therefore it is a best practice to implement type checks like this:

C++

```
if (!argument.isBool()) {
  throw JSError(runtime, "Invalid Type: expected boolean");
}
bool b = argument.getBool();
```

Sample 7.26: manual type checking exception in native code

When using this paradigm, you can handle incompatible native type errors easily in TypeScript.

Take for example this JSI function declaration:

TypeScript

```
const exampleFunction = (param: bool) => void;
```

Sample 7.27: Function declaration with string parameter

If we call exampleFunction() with a number parameter, the JSI code will throw a JSError when it discovers that the incoming argument fails .isBool().

TypeScript

```
const onPress = () => {
    exampleFunction(123); // throws Error
}
```

Sample 7.28: Function declaration with string parameter

Because of the thrown JSError on an invalid type, the JavaScript exampleFuntion(123) will reports the error, like this:

Console

```
Error: Invalid Type: expected boolean
```

Sample 7.29: Error provided when incompatible type is sent to function

In this way, the React Native developer will receive the error at runtime if they send an incompatible type as a function argument in a JSI function. Failing to do so will result in an application crash and with no explanation why there was an issue.

Accepts Primitive Type Parameters

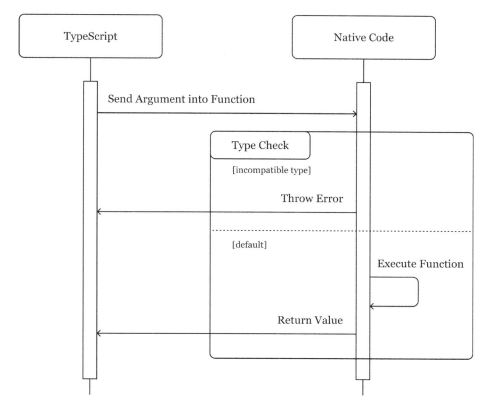

Figure 7.1: Diagram showing error when sending wrong type to function

8

Function 5: Accepts Multiple Parameters

Many times you will want to send multiple parameters to a function, for example a function that sums two numbers.

TypeScript

```
const sum = (a: number, b: number) => {
  return a + b;
}
```

Sample 8.1: Typescript implementation of a function that adds two numbers

In such a case, it is necessary to support more than one function parameter.

The lambda function parameter of `createFromHostFunction()` contains a `Value` array representing the parameters as well as a `count` representing the number of parameters in the array. Therefore it is easy to process an arbitrary number of parameters passed into a JSI function by iterating over the `Value` array.

To see this in action, let's implement the `sum()` method using JSI.

The TypeScript function declaration will be as follows:

Resulting TypeScript Function Definition:

```
const sum = (a: number, b: number) => number;
```

Sample 8.2: function declaration for tow-parameter sum method

To implement this function in JSI, we need to:

1. Verify that two parameters have been passed to the function,

2. Convert the two parameters to native `double` types,

3. Return the sum as a `facebook::jsi:Value` object.

The implementation is as follows:

C++

```
Function returnObject = Function::createFromHostFunction(... {
  if (count < 2) {
    // throw error
  }
  double a = arguments[0].toNumber();
  double b = arguments[1].toNumber();
  return Value(a + b);
}
```

Example 8.1: Two-parameter sum method implemented in JSI

If you attempt to access an argument that doesn't exist, the native code will crash with a stack overflow error. This can happen for example if you create a JSI function that requires some number of parameters but you call it from TypeScript with too few arguments, for example:

JSI Function Definition

```
Function concatenate = Function::createFromHostFunction(... {
  string s1 = arguments[0].toString().utf8();
  string s2 = arguments[1].toString().utf8();
  string output = a + " " + b;
  return Value(
    runtime,
    String.createFromUtf8(runtime, output)
  );
}
// resulting function definition:
// const concatenate = (s1: string, s2: string) -> string;
```

Sample 8.3: Creating a two-parameter string concatenate function

TypeScript call

```
concatenate("hello");
```

Sample 8.4: Calling a two-parameter function with one argument

In many cases you will want to loop over the arguments, in which case it is useful to know how many arguments have been passed into the function at runtime. This is done by accessing the last parameter of the lambda function, size_t count:

C++

```
HostFunctionType simplePrintLambda = [](
  Runtime &runtime,
  const Value &thisValue,
  const Value *arguments,
  size_t count
) -> Value {
  for (int i = 0; i < count; i++) {
    Value& argument = arguments[i];
    // work with argument
  }
  // return value
}
```

Example 8.2: Iterating over runtime parameters

Note: although it is not a good practice, it is possible to create functions which accept an arbitrary number of parameters. In this case, the number of parameters and the number of arguments passed to the function may be different.

Putting it All Together

By combining these principles, we can create the sum() function described earlier in the chapter. We will throw an error if the number of arguments is less than two and then sum the arguments to return the total. We will see more about throwing errors in Chapter 17 :

C++

```cpp
Function sumFunc = Function::createFromHostFunction(... {
  if (count < 2) {
    throw JSError(runtime, "Invalid argument count");
  }
  double total = 0.0;
  for (int i = 0; i < count; i++) {
    total += arguments[i].toNumber();
  }
  return Value(total);
}
```

Example 8.3: Looping over the number arguments to sum the values

Before using this function, you must declare it in your global context:

TypeScript

```typescript
declare global {
  function sum(a: number, b: number): number;
}
```

Sample 8.3: Declaring a JSI function in TypeScript

We can then call the sum() function from React Native like this:

TypeScript

```
const onPress = () => {
    const result: number = sum(1, 2);
    console.log("result", result); // result 3
}
```

Sample 8.4: Calling the sum() method from React Native

9

Function 6: Returns an Array

It may be that you need to return an array of data, such as a list of strings, a list of numbers, or a mixed set of data. Doing this enables you to send data that is useful for lists, searching, and statistical analysis.

Take for example a TypeScript function that returns an array of `strings`:

Resulting TypeScript Function Definition

```
const exampleFunction = () => string[];
```

Sample 9.1: Function returns an array of strings

Or a function which returns an array of `numbers`:

Resulting TypeScript Function Definition

```
const exampleFunction = () => number[];
```

Sample 9.2: Function returns an array of numbers

Or a function which returns an array that can contain a mix of `strings`, `numbers`, `null`, `undefined`, or other data types:

Resulting TypeScript Function Definition

```
const exampleFunction = () => any[];
```

Sample 9.3: Function returns an array of numbers

With functions such as these, it is then possible to loop through the result to perform some action on each element of the array.

TypeScript

```
const stringArray: string[] = exampleFunction();
for (const s of stringArray) {
  console.log(s);
}
```

Sample 9.4: Function returns an array of numbers

JSI Implementation

In these cases, we must construct a facebook::jsi::Array and populate it with Values.

The Array must be initialized with a fixed length, in this example 100 items:

C++

```
unsigned int numItems = 100;
facebook::jsi::Array exampleArray(runtime, numItems);
```

Sample 9.5: Instantiate an Array of fixed length

Then each position in the Array can be set as a Value using the .setValueAtIndex() method:

C++

```
exampleArray.setValueAtIndex(runtime, index, value);
```

Sample 9.6: Instantiate an Array of fixed length

Returns an Array

The Value can be any type, as shown before. For example String, null, number, undefined, or even an Array or Object.

For example, here is how to set a String at array index 0:

C++

```
String stringValue = String::createFromUtf8(runtime, "Hello");
exampleArray.setValueAtIndex(runtime, 0, stringValue);
// arr[0] = "Hello"
```

Sample 9.7: Add a String to the Array

Here is how to set a number at array index 1:

C++

```
String numberValue = Value(32);
exampleArray.setValueAtIndex(runtime, 1, numberValue);
// arr[1] = 32;
```

Sample 9.8: Add a number to the Array

Here is how to set null at array index 2:

C++

```
String nullValue = Value();
exampleArray.setValueAtIndex(runtime, 2, nullValue);
// arr[2] = null
```

Sample 9.9: Add a null value to the Array

Here is how to set undefined at index 3:

C++

```
String undefinedValue = Value::undefined();
exampleArray.setValueAtIndex(runtime, 3, undefinedValue);
// arr[3] = undefined
```

Sample 9.10: Add an undefined value to the Array

Here is how to build a single element array, [1] and set it as element 4:

C++

```
Array arrayValue(runtime, 1);
arrayValue.setValueAtIndex(runtime, 0, Value(1));
// [1]
exampleArray.setValueAtIndex(runtime, 4, Value(arrayValue));
// arr[4] = [1]
```

Sample 9.11: Add an array value to the Array

To return the Array, you must put it into a Value. All data exchanged with JavaScript data is packaged as the facebook:jsi::Value type.

C++

```
return Value(runtime, exampleArray);
```

Sample 9.12: Return the Array as a JavaScript Value

The resulting array from these methods will look like this in TypeScript:

TypeScript

```
const result: any[] = [
  "Hello",
  32,
  null,
  undefined,
  [1]
];
```

Sample 9.13: The result of populating the example array

Putting It All Together

Let's say we have a function called listFruit() that returns a list of fruit names: apple, banana, kiwi…. The function declaration for such a function may look like this:

TypeScript

```
const listFruit = () => string[];
```

Sample 9.14: Function declaration for a fruit listing function

We can implement a trivial fruit listing function in C++ using a static array of fruit names. In C++, there are several ways to implement this, but we will use a vector of strings. Using vectors is a way of working with array-like data without worrying about memory leaks and stack overflow errors.

In this case, we create a static `vector` of fruit names, then initialize the `facebook::jsi::Array`. We iterate over fruit names `vector` to populate each item in the `Array`, then return the `Array` as a `Facebook::jsi::Value`:

C++

```
Function listFruit = Function::createFromHostFunction(..., {
  // define a static list of fruit names
  std::vector<std::string> fruit = {
    "apple", "banana", "kiwi", "cherry"
  };

  // Create a new JSI Array with the size of the std::vector
  Array jsiFruitArray(runtime, fruit.size());

  // Populate the JSI Array with strings from the std::vector
  for (size_t i = 0; i < fruit.size(); ++i) {
    // Convert each std::string to a JSI String
    jsiFruitArray.setValueAtIndex(
      runtime,
      i,
      String::createFromUtf8(runtime, fruit[i])
    );
  }
  // return the Array as a JSI Value
  return Value(runtime, jsiFruitArray);
});
```

Example 9.1: Return an string array of fruit names

Note that we covert the native `string` type to a `facebook::jsi::String` type when setting the array item because the JSI String data type is not compatible with `std::string`.

Declare this function in the `global` context so that it calling it doesn't throw any errors:

TypeScript

```
declare global {
  function listFruit(): string[];
}
```

Sample 9.15: Declaring a JSI function in TypeScript

We can call this method from JavaScript with the following result:

TypeScript

```
const fruits: string[] = listFruit();
console.log(
  `found ${fruits.length} fruits: ${fruits.join(", ")}`
);
// found 4 fruits: apple, banana, kiwi, cherry
```

Sample 9.16: Resulting function call and output from `listFruit()` function

10

Function 7: Returns an Object

One of the features that makes TypeScript a truly great functional language is the ability to pass objects as function arguments. This allows us to send complex data into a function, often with the ability to support optional data and flexible types.

This feature makes it possible to work with complex data in a way that is readable and less error-prone than hand-setting many properties of a mutated object or passing an arbitrary number of arguments into a function.

Take for example a `Person` type, which defines a name, age, gender, and a unique identifier.

TypeScript

```typescript
type Person {
  id: string;
  name: string;
  age: number;
  gender: "male" | "female";
};
```

Sample 10.1: A simple person type with example properties

> *Note: This Person type is simple for the purpose of teaching a programming concept. A real-world application would likely have much more complex data, including multiple names, a birthday instead of an age, and possibly other changes.*

In TypeScript, a typical operation might be to retrieve Person data from a data source, such as a database or REST API.

Ignoring asynchronous calls for now, the declaration for a function that retrieves a Person object might look like this:

TypeScript function definition for a Person lookup

```
const getPersonById = (id: string) => Person;
```

Sample 10.2: TypeScript function returns Person object

Underneath, JavaScript treats the Person as a more generic object, so the actual non-TypeScript declaration should be thought of more like this:

JavaScript function definition for a Person lookup

```
const getPersonById = (id: string) => object;
```

Sample 10.3: JavaScript function returns Person object

This is a subtle but important distinction because JSI knows the object type, but is unaware of custom TypeScript types we define in the React Native code.

Creating and Returning Objects

JavaScript Native Interface can create a JavaScript-compatible `object` type by declaring a `facebook::jsi::Object`, for example this one named `yourObject`:

C++

```
Object yourObject(runtime);
```

Sample 10.4:Declare a JavaScript Object type in JSI

Once the object is created, any data type can be attached to it as a key/value pair, using the `yourObject.setProperty()` method. The `setProperty()` method takes a `std::string` as the key and `facebook::jsi::String` or any other primitive type as the value, like this:

C++

```
yourObject.setProperty(runtime, key, value);
```

Sample 10.5: Set an object property and value

As with any return, you must convert the `Object` to a `Value` like this:

C++

```
return Value(runtime, yourObject);
```

Sample 10.6: Return a Value version of the Object

Setting a String Property

To set a property as a JavaScript string type, use the String::createFromUtf8() or String::createFromAscii() method shown in Chapter 5. In this example, we are setting the stringProperty property to "Hello World";

C++

```
String s = String::createFromUtf8(runtime, "Hello World");
yourObject.setProperty(runtime, "stringProperty", s);
// yourObject.stringProperty = "Hello World"
```

Sample 10.7: Set a string value for an object property

Setting a Numeric Property

To set a property to a JavaScript number type, simply pass a number as the parameter. As JavaScript makes no distinction between floating-point and integer number types, you can pass int, float, or double into the .setProperty().

C++

```
int number = 123;
yourObject.setProperty(runtime, "intProperty", number);
// yourObject.intProperty = 123;
```

Sample 10.8: Set a number value for an object property

Setting a Null property

To set a property to a JavaScript null type, simply pass NULL as the value parameter.

C++

```
yourObject.setProperty(runtime, "nullProperty", NULL);
// yourProperty.nullProperty = null
```

Sample 10.9: Set a null value for an object property

Setting an Undefined Property

To set a property to a JavaScript undefined type, simply pass a Value::undefined() as the value.

C++

```
yourObject.setProperty(runtime, "unknown", Value::undefined);
// yourProperty.unknownProperty = undefined
```

Sample 10.10: Set an undefined value for an object property

Setting an Array Property

To set a property to an array type, you must create an facebook::jsi::Array with a known length, then populate it with data by looking over the items and assigning each element a value.

Array elements accept the same data types Object properties, so you can set facebook::jsi::String, int, double, null or Value::undefined() element types.

The Array is not strongly typed, so the element types don't need to match each other. For example, element 0 can be a String and element 1 can be a number:

C++

```
Array props(runtime, 1); // 1 element array
// set element to a JavaScript String
props.setValueAtIndex(
  runtime,
  0, // 0th element
  String::createFromUtf8(runtime, "Hello World")
);
yourObject.setProperty(runtime, "arrayProperty", props);
// yourProperty.arrayProperty = ["Hello World"]
```

Sample 10.11: Set an array value for an object property

Setting an Object Property

To set a property to a JavaScript object type, you can use the same techniques described earlier in this chapter to create an object and set its properties. Then set the property of the parent object to the new object:

C++

```
Object subObject(runtime);
subObject.setProperty(runtime, "id", Value(123));
yourObject.setProperty(runtime, "objectProperty", subObject);
// yourObject.objectProperty = { id: 123 }
```

Sample 10.12: Set an object value for an object property

Putting it All Together

Using the getPersonById() JSI function and the example Person type described earlier in the chapter, let's implement a trivial function that returns a Person matching the id 123.

In our example, let's assume Person 123 has the following shape:

Object Shape of Person 123 in TypeScript

```
{
  "id": "123",
  "name": "John Doe",
  "age": 32,
  "gender": "male"
}
```

Sample 10.13: Example object describing Person with id 123

In order to return a complex TypeScript object in JSI, we must instantiate an Object class, then set the properties one by one to return a JSON-style object.

In this implementation, we get the id parameter and return null if it doesn't match 123. Otherwise we build the Person described above and return that object as a Value.

C++

```
Function getPersonFunc = Function::createFromHostFunction(... {
  // get the first argument as a string
  string id = arguments[0].getString(runtime).utf8(
    runtime
  );
  // return null if id the id isn't "123"
  if (id != "123") {
    return Value();
  }
  // build an object
  Object personObject(runtime);
  String name = String::createFromUtf8(runtime, "John Doe");
  int age = 32;
  String gender = String::createFromUtf8(runtime, "male");
  // set the object properties
  personObject.setProperty(runtime, "id", id);
  personObject.setProperty(runtime, "name", name);
  personObject.setProperty(runtime, "age", age);
  personObject.setProperty(runtime, "gender", gender);
  // return the object
  return Value(runtime, personObject);
});
```

Example 10.1: Return a Person when the id parameter is 123

Don't forget to declare the function with the proper return type in your global context to make the TypeScript compiler knows the function exists and the code editor knows what properties to expect in the returned object:

TypeScript

```
declare global {
  function getPersonById(id: string): Person;
}
```

Sample 10.14: Declaring a JSI function in TypeScript

11

Function 8: Accepts Mixed Types for a Parameter

Function parameters are a source of potential complexity and errors when executing JSI functions from TypeScript because of both the difference in native types between TypeScript and C++, but also because TypeScript types are actually objects which can be `null` or `undefined`, and may even be arrays or complex object types, such as the `Person` object described in Chapter 10.

In TypeScript, defining mixed types for function parameters is fairly easy, for example this function that takes one parameter which can be a `string`, `number`, `null`, or `undefined`:

Resulting TypeScript Function Definition

```
const exampleFunction = (
  parameter: string | number | null | undefined
) => void;
```

Sample 11.1: Function accepts primitive types as a parameter

Since C++ uses strict typing, it is difficult to accept arbitrarily-typed arguments in native functions. This is where the `facebook:jsi::Value` type comes in handy as a container for arbitrary types.

As we've seen before, we can test if a `Value` contains a JavaScript type such as a `string`, `number`, `null`, `undefined`:

C++

```
const Value &argument = arguments[0];
bool isString = argument.isString();
```

Sample 11.2: Test if a parameter is one of several types

Once we know what type the parameter is, we can convert the `Value` to a native type, for example an `std::string`:

C++

```
string stringValue = argument.getString(runtime).utf8(runtime);
```

Sample 11.3: Convert the parameter to a native string

Let's see how to implement an arbitrary type parameter in JavaScript Native Interface.

JSI Implementation

In TypeScript, if you pass the wrong type into a function, the compiler will typically complain about a Type Error, for example this one produced when sending a number into a function that expects a `string` argument:

TypeScript

```
const exampleFunction = (parameter: string): void => {
  console.log(parameter);
}
exampleFunction(123);
// Error: TS2345: Argument of type 'number'
// is not assignable to parameter of type 'string'
```

Example 11.4: Argument type mismatch error in TypeScript

We want to reproduce that behavior by accepting and processing arguments that are desired types and throwing type errors when invalid data types are sent as arguments into a JSI function.

We will do that by testing if the argument type is one of several types we want to support for that argument, and throw an error otherwise.

Determine the Type of a Parameter

The first step is to determine the type of an argument. Maybe you need to treat it differently or throw an error if the wrong type is passed for example.

Based on examples from Chapter 7, here are some examples of how to check for different types:

C++

```
Function exampleFunc = Function::createFromHostFunction(... {
  // get argument as a reference to a facebook::jsi::Value
  const Value& argument = arguments[0];
  // true if the argument is a `string`
  bool isString = argument.isString();
  // true if the argument is a `number`
  bool isNumber = argument.isNumber();
  // true if the argument is a `bool`
  bool isBool = argument.isBool();
  // true if the argument is a `null`
  bool isNull = argument.isNull();
  // true if the argument is a `undefined`
  bool isUndefined = argument.isUndefined();
  // true if the argument is an `object`
  bool isObject = argument.isObject();
  // TypeScript arrays are `object` types,
  // but can be tested separately as arrays
  bool isArray = false;
  if (isObject) {
    isArray = argument.getObject(runtime).isArray(runtime);
  }
});
```

Example 11.1: Determine the type of an argument

Retrieve the Argument as Expected Type

Once you've safely type-checked a function parameter, you can retrieve the data to the correct type without creating any runtime exceptions that will crash your program.

C++

```
Function returnObject = Function::createFromHostFunction(... {
  // get the argument as reference to facebook::jsi::Value
  Value& argument = arguments[0];
  // if argument.isString() == true, get a utf8 std::string:
  string stringVal = argument.getString(runtime).utf8(runtime);
  // if argument.isNumber() == true, get a double
  double doubleValue = argument.getNumber();
  // if argument.isBool() == true, get a bool
  bool boolValue = argument.getBool();
  // null and undefined types don't return a value
});
```

Example 11.2: Converting JavaScript data types to native types

Example: Optional String Parameter

Putting these two concepts together, we can test if an optional string parameter was passed into the example function, for example these two function calls:

TypeScript

```
// expected function definition:
// const mixedParameter = (string?) => void;
mixedParameter("example");
mixedParameter(undefined);
mixedParameter(); // similar to mixedParameter(undefined)
```

Sample 11.5: Calling a function with optional parameter

Optional parameters are default to undefined when not defined, so a JSI function that checks for optional argument values must test if the argument is undefined or if it is a string or something else.

C++

```
Function mixedParms = Function::createFromHostFunction(... {
  if (count == 0) {
    cout << "parameter was not defined" << endl;
  } else {
    // get the argument as a reference to a jsi::Value
    const Value &argument = arguments[0];
    if (argument.isString()) {
      string strVal =
argument.getString(runtime).utf8(runtime);
      cout << "parameter was a string: " << strVal << endl;
    } else if (argument.isUndefined()) {
      cout << "parameter was undefined" << endl;
    } else {
      throw JSError(runtime, "Invalid argument type");
    }
  }
  return Value::undefined();
});
```

Example 11.4: Checking for an undefined parameter in TypeScript

Don't forget to declare the function with the proper parameter types in your global context to make the TypeScript compiler knows the function exists and the code editor knows what argument types it supports:

TypeScript

```
declare global {
  function mixedParameter(
    param: string | number | null | undefined
  ): void;
}
```

Sample 11.6: Declaring a JSI function in TypeScript

12

Function 9: Accepts Objects as Parameters

TypeScript can pass complex objects as function arguments, which is a challenge to process using JSI because of not only the complexity from the previous example, but also because the object must be destructured to work with individual properties, and the parameter may accept more than one object type.

Expected TypeScript Function Definition

```
const simplePrint = (parameter: object) => void;
```

Sample 12.1: Function accepts object as a parameter

> *Note: Passing a generic object type in TypeScript is not advisable because the linter may complain that it doesn't know the object properties. It is always better to pass a defined type.*

Let's say we have a `Person` type in TypeScript which we want to work with. For the sake of simplicity, the `Person` has a name, age, and binary gender, as well as unique identifier:

TypeScript

```typescript
type Person = {
  id: string;
  name: string;
  age: number;
  gender: "male" | "female";
};
```

Sample 12.2: A simple Person type in Typescript

It is possible to pass an object of this type into a TypeScript function by declaring a function parameter as having the `Person` type. For example, we can create a function that prints a given person's name, age, and gender to the console, like this:

TypeScript

```typescript
const logPersonStats = (person: Person) => {
  console.log(
    `Person ${person.name} is a ${person.gender}, ` +
    `${person.age} years old`
  );
}
```

Sample 12.3: TypeScript function that prints a person's name and age

Calling that function requires that we build a valid `Person` object and pass it as a parameter into the `logPersonStats()` function, like this:

TypeScript

```
const person: Person = {
  id: "123",
  name: "John Doe",
  age: 32,
  gender: "male"
};
logPersonStats(person);
// Person John Doe is a male, 32 years old
```

Sample 12.4: Create a `Person` object and pass into a function

Because `logPersonStats()` function requires a `Person` object as the first parameter, TypeScript will complain if we pass another data type into the function, for example if we try to send a number as the function argument:

TypeScript

```
logPersonStats(123);
// Error: Argument of type 'number'
// is not assignable to parameter of type 'Person'.
```

Sample 12.5: Passing incompatible type to function in TypeScript

Let's see how to implement a similar function in JavaScript Native Interface that takes a specific object type parameter.

JSI Implementation

As we have seen before, it is possible to get the JavaScript-compatible Object variable from a facebook::jsi::Value parameter using the .getObject() method.

C++

```
const Object &person = arguments[0].getObject(runtime);
```

Sample 12.6: Get the Object from the function parameter

JSI is blind to types defined in the TypeScript code. Types are defined in TypeScript and the JSI is defined in C++, each side totally unaware of how the other works. For this reason, JSI can only understand that the Person sent into the function is a generic Object type.

If the passed in argument is not a valid Object, the function will throw an error, similar to the example above.

It is possible to check if an Value is an Object, which may be useful in cases where the parameter supports multiple types:

C++

```
boolean isObject = arguments[0].isObject(runtime);
```

Sample 12.7: Check if an argument is an Object type

Javascript Arrays and Functions show up as Object types also, so this check will return true even if the argument is not really an object. For this reason, you may also want to check if the resulting Object is not an Array and not a Function.

To test if the argument is a true object type and not a function or array, it may useful to explicitly test for these cases by retrieving the `Object` and checking the result of `.isArray()` and `.isFunction()`:

C++

```
boolean isObject = arguments[0].isObject(runtime);
const Object &objectRef = arguments[0].getObject(runtime);
isObject &&= !objectRef.isArray() && !objectRef.isFunction();
```

Sample 12.8: Check if the argument is a non-array, non-function object

Chapter 13 and 15 show how to work with array and function arguments in more detail.

Once the `Object` has been retrieved, it is possible to extract properties from the object, in this case the name, age, and gender.

We start by using the `.getProperty()` method to get a property of the `Object`:

C++

```
const Value &idProperty = person.getProperty(runtime, "id");
```

Sample 12.8: Get a property from the `Object`

Once the property has been isolated, it is possible to retrieve the data within it using methods we've seen before. For example, to extract a `string`, we use the `.getString()` method:

C++

```
string id = idProperty.getString(runtime).utf8(runtime);
```

Sample 12.9: Get a string from an `Object` property

To get the age as an integer, we can get the age property from the person, get it's number value, then cast it as an int:

C++

```
int age = static_cast<int>(
  person.getProperty(runtime, "age").getNumber()
);
```

Sample 12.10: Retrieve a number and cast it as an integer

If the .getString() or .getNumber() methods find the wrong type in that property, they will throw type mismatch errors, helping to ensure that the object passed in takes the expected shape.

Any properties not checked will not trigger an error, so the person object can contain any random properties not defined in the TypeScript type, for example a mood or a birthday.

One way to ensure stricter checking of the shape of an Object is to count the number of properties to ensure it is less than some max, for example:

C++

```
std::vector<PropNameID> propertyNames =
  arguments[0].getPropertyNames(runtime);
unsigned int numProperties = propertyNames.size(runtime);
```

Sample 12.11: Count the number of properties in an Object

The Person object for example should have exactly 4 properties, so we could choose to throw a type error if the argument has fewer or more properties. We will learn more about throwing errors in Chapter 17.

C++

```
if (numProperties != 4) {
  // throw error
}
```

Sample 12.12: Ensure that a Person object has strictly 4 properties

Example: Logging a Person to Console

Putting these concepts together, we can receive a Person object into a JSI function and print its data to the console:

C++

```
Function logPersonStats = Function::createFromHostFunction(...
  // get the first argument as an facebook::jsi::Object
  const Object &person = arguments[0].getObject(runtime);
  string id = person.getProperty(
    runtime, "id"
  ).getString(runtime).utf8(runtime);
  string name = person.getProperty(
    runtime, "name"
  ).getString(runtime).utf8(runtime);
  string gender = person.getProperty(
    runtime, "gender"
  ).getString(runtime).utf8(runtime);
  int age = static_cast<int>(
    person.getProperty(runtime, "age").getNumber()
  );
  cout << "Person " << name << " is a " << gender << ", ";
  cout << age << " years old" << endl;
});
```

Example 12.1: Deconstruct a Person argument passed to a function

The result is a function with the following signature, which is as close as we can get in JSI to the `logPersonStats()` method described earlier in the chapter:

C++

```
const logPersonStats = (person: object) => void;
```

Sample 12.13: Resulting JSI function signature

But just as before, if we call this function in TypeScript using a `Person` object, it will print the person's information to a console:

C++

```
logPersonStats(person);
// Person John Doe is a male, 32 years old
```

Sample 12.14: Calling the JSI `logPersonStats()` function logs to console

Note: Remember that the JSI console may not be the same as the React Native console. Be sure to check your Xcode log, Android Log, or other logging outputs to see where JSI logs information on your system.

And of course passing the wrong type will result in a TypeScript error:

C++

```
logPersonStats(123);
// Error: Argument of type 'number'
// is not assignable to parameter of type 'Object'.
```

Sample 12.15: Passing incorrect type to JSI function will result in an error.

Don't forget to declare the function with the proper parameter type in your global context to make the TypeScript compiler knows the function exists and the code editor knows what argument types it supports:

TypeScript

```
declare global {
    function logPersonStats(person: Person): void;
}
```

Sample 12.7: Declaring a JSI function in TypeScript

13

Function 10: Accepts Arrays as Parameters

Arrays in TypeScript are a little strange. Even though they are declared using square brackets ([]), internally they are seen as object types.

Take for example a function that takes a string array as a parameter, then logs the parameter type, we will see that the console reports that the argument is an object:

TypeScript

```
const logArrayType(arr: string[]) {
  console.log(`arr is an "${typeof arr}" type`);
}
logArrayType(["one", "one", "three"]);
// arr is an "object" type
```

Sample 13.1: Function showing that arrays are objects in TypeScript

This strange behavior is because although TypeScript provides type-hinting in the editor, it gets executed as regular JavaScript, which has a simpler type system, and because arrays in JavaScript actually are objects, complete with a length property, and .push() and .append() methods.

However arrays and objects don't behave the same. The `string[]` type is not the same as another object type such as a `Person` which is why when trying to find the first element of a `person` object will throw an error. A `Person` doesn't have a `.0` property:

TypeScript

```
console.log(person[0]);
// Error: Property '0' does not exist on type 'Person'
```

Sample 13.2: Arrays and other objects are not interchangeable

Similarly, if trying to find the `.length` property of a `person` object will throw an error. A `Person` doesn't have a `.length` property:

TypeScript

```
console.log(person.length);
// Error: Property 'length' does not exist on type 'Person'
```

Sample 13.4: Arrays and other objects are not interchangeable

Of course there are ways to make an array and an object seem compatible in TypeScript, but in general they are not compatible types.

For these reasons, we must retrieve the `facebook::jsi::Array` from an `Object`, rather than directly from the `Value` the in JSI:

C++

```
const Array &arr = arguments[0].getObject(runtime)
  .getArray(runtime);
```

Sample 13.5: get the Array from a function parameter

If the argument is not an object or not an array type, then this function will throw an error, similar to the samples we saw above.

If you want your function to be flexible enough to handle arrays and other types, you may want to test if the parameter is an array type as opposed to a Function or any other object type, like this:

C++

```
const Object &obj = arguments[0].getObject(runtime);
boolean isArray = obj.isArray(runtime);
```

Sample 13.6: Check if a function parameter is an array

The Array object in an object with its own properties and methods, including the .size() method which functions like TypeScript's .length property. Therefore, you can get the length of an Array by executing its .size() method:

C++

```
size_t numElements = arr.size(runtime);
```

Sample 13.7: Get the length of a JSI Array.

Once you have the Array, you can work with it as such, for example iterate over items:

C++

```
size_t numElements = array.size(runtime);
for (size_t i = 0; i < numElements; ++i) {
  // do something with array element i
}
```

Sample 13.8: iterate over a JSI Array

Just as with object properties, each `Array` element is a `Value` type, which you can isolate using the array's `.getValueAtIndex()` method:

C++

```
Value element = arr.getValueAtIndex(runtime, i);
```

Sample 13.9: Get array element at position i

If you try to get the array value of an index that is outside the bounds of the array, an error will be thrown. For example, accessing the nth+1 element of the array like this:

C++

```
Value element = arr.getValueAtIndex(runtime, numElements);
```

Sample 13.10:

Will result in a mysterious error in React Native that reminds us which JavaScript engine is running:

Console

```
Error: , js engine: hermes
```

Sample 13.11: Error from accessing invalid array element

Once the element is isolated, it can be treated as any other `Value` object, and converted to a `string`, `double`, `boolean`, `null`, or anything else as needed.

JSI Implementation

Let's say we have a function called `logFruitArray()` that takes an array of JavaScript `strings` and prints the array length and each fruit name to the console in order, like this:

TypeScript

```
const fruit = ["apple", "banana", "kiwi", "cherry"];
logFruitArray(fruit);
// 4 fruit found
// - apple
// - banana
// - kiwi
// - cherry
```

Sample 13.13: Log fruit names tho the console using a function

Such a function would be declared like this in TypeScript:

Resulting TypeScript Function Definition

```
const logFruitArray = (fruit: string[]) => void;
```

Sample 13.14: Function accepts an array as a parameter

The JSI implementation for such a function would look like this, converting the function argument to an array, counting the number of items, then looping over each array item, converting to a String and printing the result to the console:

C++

```
Function logFruitArray = Function::createFromHostFunction(... {
  // Get the JSI Array from the Value
  const Array &fruit = arguments[0].getObject(runtime)
    .getArray(runtime);
  // Get the length of the array
  size_t length = fruit.size(runtime);
  cout << length << " fruit found:" << endl;
  // Iterate over the array element
  for (size_t i = 0; i < length; ++i) {
    // Get the ith element in the array
    const Value &element = fruit.getValueAtIndex(runtime, i);
    // Convert the JSI String to std::string, add it to vector
    string fruitName = element.getString(runtime).utf8(
      runtime
    );
    // log to console
    cout << "- " << fruitName << endl;
  }
});
```

Example 13.1: JSI Function logs fruit names and array length to console

Don't forget to declare the function so that calling it doesn't cause a problem:

TypeScript

```
declare global {
  function logFruitArray(fruit: string[]): void;
}
```

Sample 13.15: Declaring a JSI function in TypeScript

14

Function 11: Returns a Promise

Sometimes executing a function takes an indeterminate amount of time, such as URL queries, database lookups, and generating machine learning content.

In TypeScript, these types of functions are typically executed through asynchronous functions, also known as Promises.

An asynchronous, or async function definition that typically looks like this, where the function is both declared with the async keyword and returns a Promise resolving to type, in this case a method that converts an number to a string:

TypeScript

```
const toString = async (number: number) => Promise<string>;
```

Sample 14.1: Asynchronous function declaration, returning a string

It is useful to know that an asynchronous function in TypeScript is implemented using a `Promise` object, which has one method `.resolve()` to return a value and one method `.reject()` to handle a failure:

TypeScript

```typescript
const toString = async (number: number) => Promise<string> {
  return new Promise((resolve, reject) => {
    setTimeout(() => resolve("Promise succeeded"), 100);
    reject(new Error("Promise failed"));
  });
}
```

Sample 14.2: Simple `Promise` implementation in TypeScript

Although JavaScript supports asynchronous function calls, Today's JavaScript engines are single-threaded. This means that all code is executed in sequence, sometimes resulting in apps that feel laggy.

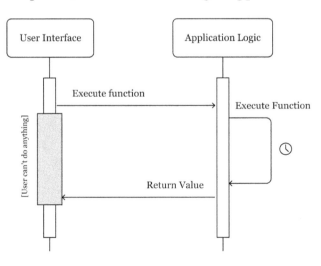

Figure 14.1: Single-thread execution creates delays in user interaction

However, methods that are called from TypeScript aren't required to run on the same thread. This is one of the superpowers of JavaScript Native Interface: C++ can be used to create multi-threaded applications that take advantage of the multiple CPU cores available on modern computers and smartphones. This can leave the main thread free to focus on user-interface updates such as animations while other tasks can be done in parallel.

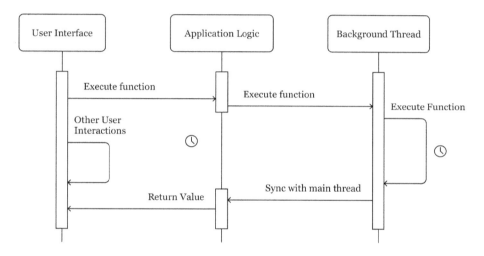

Figure 14.2: Parallel execution creates a smoother user experience

The way asynchronous functions are expressed have changed several times in the last few years as JavaScript and TypeScript have evolved as languages.

You may recognize the older, Promise-based implementation:

TypeScript

```
asyncFunction().then(result => {
  console.log(`result: ${result}`);
});
```

Sample 14.3: Calling an asynchronous function using `.then()`

If the async function supports a failure response, this implementation may include an `.error()` function also:

TypeScript

```
asyncFunction()
  .then(result => console.log(`result: ${result}`))
  .error(error => console.error(e.message));
```

Sample 14.4: Calling an asynchronous function using .then() and .error()

However the modern way to call an asynchronous function is to use the await keyword, like this:

TypeScript

```
const result = await asyncFunction();
console.log(`result: ${result}`);
```

Sample 14.5: Calling an asynchronous function using await

This style of calling an async function allows us clearly assign variables and constants even in situations where it is unclear how long a function might take to complete.

If the async function supports an error response, this implementation uses a try / catch block to catch the error:

TypeScript

```
try {
  const result = await asyncFunction();
  console.log(`result: ${result}`);
} catch (error: any) {
  console.log(e.message);
}
```

Sample 14.6: Calling an async function using await *and catching errors*

JSI Implementation

In Javascript Native Interface, we create an asynchronous function by creating and returning a promise:

C++

```
// construct the promise
Function promiseConstructor = runtime.global()
  .getPropertyAsFunction(runtime, "Promise");

// create the promise logic and return the promise
return promiseConstructor.callAsConstructor(
  runtime, Function::createFromHostFunction(
    runtime,
    PropNameID::forAscii(runtime, "executor"),
    2, // takes two arguments: resolve and reject
    [](
      Runtime &runtime,
      const Value &thisVal,
      const Value *promiseArgs,
      size_t count
    ) -> Value {
      // actual Promise logic here
    }
  );
  // note that the promise itself returns `undefined`
  return Value::undefined();
);
```

Sample 14.7: Returning the Promise

Inside the Promise, we can get the two arguments, resolve and reject, both of which are callback functions:

C++

```cpp
const Function &resolve = promiseArgs[0].getObject(runtime)
  .getFunction(runtime);
const Function &reject = promiseArgs[1].getObject(runtime)
  .getFunction(runtime);
```

Sample 14.8: Get the resolve and reject callbacks

Then to call resolve the promise, pass any JSI-compatible data into the resolve function. In this example we resolve the Promise to an facebook::jsi::String containing the text hello:

C++

```cpp
String result = String::createFromUtf8(runtime, "hello");
resolve.call(runtime, result);
```

Sample 14.9: Resolve a promise

To handle an error, pass any JSI-compatible data into the `reject` callback. In this example, we get the create a new `facebook::jsi::String` from the `std::exception` to describe the error type:

C++

```
try {
  100 / 0; // do something that triggers an exception
} catch (const std::exception &e) {
  reject.call(
    runtime,
    String::createFromUtf8(runtime, e.what())
  );
}
```

Sample 14.10: Reject the Promise

Example: Get a Person By Id

Putting these concepts together, we can implement a simple asynchronous function that acts like a database lookup, taking a `string` id and returning a `promise` that resolves to a `string`.

The definition signature for such a function might be like this:

Expected Function Definition

```
const getUserNameFromId = async (
  userId: string
) => Promise<string>;
```

Sample 14.11: Function signature for async method that returns a Person

Our user name lookup implementation will be trivial, simply comparing the incoming userId to static strings and returning a corresponding name:

C++

```cpp
string getUserNameFromIdNative(
  Runtime& runtime, string userId
) {
  string name;
  if (userId == "123") {
    name = "John";
  } else if (userId == "124") {
    name = "Jane";
  } else {
    throw JSError(runtime, "User not found");
  }
  return name;
}
```

Sample 14.12: User name lookup algorithm

To use the result of the getUserNameFromStringNative() function in a JSI Promise, we must create a Promise, get the userId parameter as a string, then return the result of the function in the resolve.call() method. We handle any exceptions as reject.call() and we return undefined to the Promise:

C++

```
Function getPersonById = Function::createFromHostFunction(...,{
  Function promiseConstructor = runtime.global()
    .getPropertyAsFunction(runtime, "Promise");
  Value promise = promiseConstructor.callAsConstructor(
    runtime, Function::createFromHostFunction(
      runtime, PropNameID::forAscii(runtime, "executor"
    ),
    2, // resolve and reject
    [ userId = arguments[0].getString(runtime).utf8(runtime) ](
      Runtime &runtime, const Value &thisVal,
      const Value *promiseArgs, size_t count
    ) -> Value {
      // get resolve and reject from the arguments
      const Function &resolve = promiseArgs[0].getObject(
        runtime).getFunction(runtime);
      const Function &reject = promiseArgs[1].getObject(
        runtime).getFunction(runtime);
      try {
        string name = getUserNameFromIdNative(runtime, userId);
        resolve.call(
          runtime, String::createFromUtf8(runtime, name));
      } catch (const std::runtime_error& e) {
        reject.call(
          runtime, String::createFromUtf8(runtime, e.what()));
      }
      return Value::undefined();
    });
  return promise;
});
```

Example 14.1: Returning user name as a promise from an external function

Don't forget to declare the function. Notice that the declaration does not contain an `async` keyword, but it does return a `Promise` with the `string` type resolution:

TypeScript

```
declare global {
    function getUserNameFromId(userId: string): Promise<string>;
}
```

Sample 14.12: Declaring a JSI function in TypeScript

15

Function 12: Accepts Callback Functions as Parameters

Similar to Promises, Callback functions are a way to execute asynchronous code in TypeScript. They are commonly used to define what happens when an event occurs, such as a button click or a URL request finishes executing. They help to make code that can trigger and cancel events regardless of when or where the event happens, or how long an algorithm takes to execute.

You may recognize the following pattern the setTimeout() method, which executes a callback after so many milliseconds:

TypeScript

```
setTimeout(() => {
  console.log(`Task executed after 1000 ms`);
}, 1000);
```

Sample 15.1: Using setTimeout() callback

In this example, the setTimeout() function executes a callback after the timeout occurs, similar to an asynchronous function. You can think of setTimeout() as having the following method declaration:

TypeScript

```
const setTimeout = (
  callback: () => void,
  timeout: number
) => void;
```

Sample 15.2: SetTimeout method declaration

The callback parameter is a function, so in this case you are passing a function as an argument into a function.

In fact, React Native uses this pattern a lot, since it uses callback events to trigger UI updates. Functions such as useEffect(), useCallback(), and useMemo() all take callback functions as arguments, which are executed in response to a change in the system state.

Take for example React Native's useEffect() function, which takes a function as it's first parameter and an array of variables as the second. useEffect() triggers the callback any time one of the dependent variables is updated.

TypeScript

```
const useEffect = (
  setup: () => void,
  dependencies: any[]
) => void;
```

Sample 15.3: Simplified function definition for useEffect()

In fact, even the JSX code that executes functions on button press and other events in React Native are actually callback functions, just written with a different syntax:

TypeScript JSX

```
<button
  title="Press me"
  onPress={() => {
    console.log("Button pressed")
  }}
/>
```

Sample 15.4: Event-driven callback written in JSX

In this sample, the callback function is executed each time the user presses the button.

With these examples, we see that callback methods can be used to help make code that is asynchronous, reactive, and event-driven.

For context, here is how we would create a function that executes a simple callback in TypeScript:

Typescript

```
const executeCallback = (
  callbackFunction: () => void
): void => {
  callbackFunction();
}
```

Sample 15.5: Callback execution function in TypeScript

To use such a function, we would pass a callback as the callbackFunction argument:

TypeScript

```
executeCallback(() => {
  console.log("callbackFunction executed");
}
```

Sample 15.6: Execute callback execution function in TypeScript

JSI Implementation

Implementing a callback in Javascript Native Interface is straightforward, as JavaScript functions are a type of object type. This means we can get a facebook::jsi::Function directly from a facebook::jsi::Object using its .getFunction() method:

C++

```
Function callbackFunction = arguments[0]
  .getObject(runtime)
  .getFunction(runtime);
```

Sample 15.7: Get a callback function from an function parameter

If we like, we can check if the object is a function using the .isFunction() method:

C++

```
boolean callbackFunction = arguments[0]
  .getObject(runtime)
  .isFunction(runtime);
```

Sample 15.8: Determine if a parameter is a function

After we have isolated the callback function, we can execute it at any time using it's `.call()` method:

C++

```
callback.call(runtime);
```

Sample 15.9: Execute a callback function without arguments

Example: Native SetTimeout

Let's see how to implement a native `setTimeout()` function using JavaScript Native Interface. To do this, let's create a JSI function that takes two arguments, a function and a number.

Although threading in C++ is beyond the scope of this book, we can create a simple blocking delay before executing the callback:

C++

```
#include <unistd.h>

// Sleep for `timeoutMilliseconds` milliseconds
usleep(timeoutMilliseconds);
// execute callback when the timer completes
callback.call(runtime);
```

Sample 15.10: Executing a delay timer using threads in C++

Putting these together, we have a function that receives a callback function as the first parameter and a delay time as the second parameter. It sleeps for the timeout period and then executes the callback before returning undefined:

C++

```
#include <unistd.h>

Function setTimeoutNative = Function::createFromHostFunction(..
  Function callback = arguments[0]
    .getObject(runtime)
    .getFunction(runtime);
  int timeoutMilliseconds = arguments[1].getNumber();

  // Sleep for `timeoutMilliseconds` milliseconds
  usleep(timeoutMilliseconds);
  // execute callback when the timer completes
  callback.call(runtime);
  return Value::undefined();
});
```

Example 15.1: Native implementation of setTimeout() method

This results in the creation of a function with the following TypeScript function definition:

TypeScript

```
const setTimeoutNative = (
  callback: () => void,
  timeoutMilliseconds: number
) => void;
```

Sample 15.11: TypeScript function definition of setTimeoutNative()

You must declare it in the global context so that TypeScript knows that it is available:

TypeScript

```
declare global {
  function setTimeoutNative(
    callback: () => void,
    timeoutMilliseconds: number
  ): void;
}
```

Sample 15.12: Declaring a JSI function in TypeScript

Calling this method from TypeScript should look familiar, simply pass a callback function as the first argument and a millisecond timeout number as the second parameter:

TypeScript

```
setTimeoutNative(() => {
  console.log("Native timeout exceeded, callback called");
}, 1000);
// after 1000 milliseconds...
// Native timeout exceeded, callback called
```

Sample 15.13: Calling the native setTimeoutNative() method

Note: In a more real-world implementation of this function, you are likely to create a second thread to handle the callback. Threading in C++ is a little complicated and is beyond the scope of this book. In this case, you would return undefined in the main function, likely before the callback is executed.

16

Function 13: Accepts Functions with Parameters as Arguments

A callback function isn't just an event. Sometimes it must contain the result of some outcome or user action. For this reason, it can be useful when the callback functions accept parameters.

This pattern is common for example in React Native when handling the onChangeText() event from a TextInput:

TypeScript JSX

```
<TextInput
  onChangeText={(text: string) => {
    console.log(`Text: ${text}`);
  }}
/>
```

Sample 16.1: Parameterized callback function on onChangeText() event

Or if you have ever needed to know the current value of a useState()
when setting the new value, for example when implementing an
increment method:

TypeScript

```
const [count, setCount] = useState(0);
const incrementCount = () => {
  setCount(oldCount => oldCount + 1);
}
```

Sample 16.2: Incrementing a value using a callback state setter

These are both examples of callback functions that receive a
parameter. The parameter is important in knowing what the outcome
of the callback is at that moment.

Let's say we have a function called randomDelay() that executes a
callback after a random delay. The callback contains a parameter that
shows the length of the delay between calling randomDelay() and
executing the callback.

The definition of this function would be as follows:

TypeScript

```
const randomDelay = async (
  (millisecondsElapsed: number) => void
) => void;
```

Sample 16.3: Function accepts callback, which takes a parameter

We can call the `randomDelay()` function like this to print the time delay in executing the callback:

TypeScript

```
randomDelay((millisecondsElapsed: number) => {
  console.log(
    `callback executed after ${millisecondsElapsed} ms`
  );
});
// after, for example 1924 milliseconds...
// callback executed after 1924 ms
```

Sample 16.4: calling a function with a parameter in the callback

JSI Implementation

The process of isolating the callback function from the JSI function is the same as the method described in the previous chapter:

C++

```
Function callbackFunction = arguments[0]
  .getObject(runtime)
  .getFunction(runtime);
```

Sample 16.5: Isolate a callback function parameter

JavaScript Native Interface has no specific way of knowing that this function takes any specific parameters of any specific types. We can execute the callback using any Value, so it's best to create a consistent API and document your functions well for other developers.

Let's say you have created a String parameter:

C++

```
String value = String::createFromUtf8("Hello");
```

Sample 16.6: Creating a String value

You can then execute the callback by passing that value as an argument:

C++

```
callback.call(runtime, value);
```

Sample 16.7: Execute the callback with a parameter

If you have multiple parameters in your callback, you can simply call the callback with those parameters:

C++

```
callback.call(runtime, value1, value2, value3);
```

Sample 16.8: Execute callback with multiple parameters

Example: Callback After Random Delay

Let's see how to implement the `randomDelay()` function using JavaScript Native Interface. The implementation will be almost identical to the `setTimeoutNative()` function from the previous chapter, except for two things:

1. The delay time will be randomly set inside the function,

2. The callback will include the elapsed time as a parameter.

We can create a random delay time between 0 and 1000 milliseconds by creating and seeding a random number generator, then creating a distribution range and picking a random number from the range:

C++

```
int get_random_number(int low, int high) {
  random_device random_number_generator;
  mt19937 picker(random_number_generator());
  uniform_int_distribution<> distribution(low, high);
  int random_number = distribution(picker);
  return random_number;
}
```

Sample 16.9: Create a random integer

When we execute the callback function, we pass the random number as a `facebook::jsi::Value` as a parameter of the callback:

C++

```
int timeoutMilliseconds = get_random_number(0, 1000);
callback.call(runtime, Value(timeoutMilliseconds));
```

Sample 16.10: Execute the callback with an argument

If you need to return more than one parameter, you can execute the callback function with a pointer to an array of Values and the size of the array, for example like this:

C++

```
Value callbackArguments[] = { Value(1), Value(2), Value(3) };
callback.call(runtime, *callbackArguments, 3);
```

Sample 16.11: Execute the callback with multiple arguments

Putting these together, we have a function that receives a callback function as a parameter. It generates a random delay time and then runs a thread that sleeps for that number of milliseconds, then executes the callback on the main thread, passing the delay time as a parameter:

C++

```
Function randomDelay = Function::createFromHostFunction(... {
  Function callback = arguments[0]
    .getObject(runtime)
    .getFunction(runtime);
  int timeoutMilliseconds = get_random_number(0, 1000);
  // delay for some time
  usleep(timeoutMilliseconds);
  // execute the callback
  callback.call(runtime, Value(timeoutMilliseconds));
  return Value::undefined();
});
```

Example 16.1: Native implementation of setTimeout() method

This results in the creation of a function with the following TypeScript definition:

TypeScript

```
const randomDelay = (
  callback: (millisecondsElapsed: number) => void
) => void;
```

Sample 16.12: TypeScript function definition of randomDelay()

Of course the function declaration in `global` is slightly different:

TypeScript

```
declare global {
  function randomDelay(
    callback: (millisecondsElapsed: number) => void
  ): void;
}
```

Sample 16.13: Declaring a JSI function in TypeScript

Calling this method from TypeScript should look familiar, simply pass a callback function as the parameter and capture the millisecond timeout number as the callback's parameter:

TypeScript

```
randomDelay((millisecondsElapsed: number) => {
  console.log(
    `callback executed after ${millisecondsElapsed} ms`
  );
});
```

Sample 16.14: Calling the native randomDelay() function

For clarity, you can also define the callback response separately, and pass it as an argument to the randomDelay() function by name:

TypeScript

```typescript
const randomDelayCallback = (millisecondsElapsed: number) => {
  console.log(
    `callback executed after ${millisecondsElapsed} ms`
  );
});
randomDelay(randomDelayCallback);
```

Sample 16.15: Alternative method of calling randomDelay() *function*

17

Function 14: Throws Errors

In TypeScript, many times it is useful to throw an error when something goes wrong.

In general, you should assume your code will fail, and Errors provide a convenient way to diagnose how, why, and where it failed. Errors allow developers to explain what type of problem occurred in the code as well as to every line of code that contributed to or was affected by the error in the resulting stack trace.

Therefore, it is useful to throw errors, especially when writing code that crosses a language barrier. JSI functions are essentially opaque to TypeScript, meaning that without throwing descriptive Errors, there may be no way to know how, why, or even *if* a JSI function failed.

In TypeScript, we can throw an Error like this:

TypeScript

```
const throwErrorFunction = () => {
   throw new Error("This message describes what went wrong");
}
```

Sample 17.1: Throw an error in TypeScript.

This error can be caught later in the code. A polished program would handle an error using a fallback procedure or display actionable information in the user interface, but during debugging it is useful to see the stack trace:

TypeScript

```
try {
  throwErrorFunction();
} catch (error: any) {
  console.error(e.message);
  console.error(e.stack);
}
```

Sample 17.2: Catch an error and display the stack trace

A stack trace is invaluable for debugging because it shows the exact path the execution took through the program's call stack up to the point where the error occurred. This allows developers to trace back through the function calls and understand the sequence of operations that led to the error, which is critical for diagnosing and fixing issues in the code.

A stack trace depends highly on the files and method names and frameworks used in a project, but an example stack trace looks like this:

Console

```
Error: This message describes what went wrong
    at throwErrorFunction (/src/utilities/errors.ts:7:15)
    at exampleFrontEndFile (/src/ui/frontend.ts:12:23)
    at main (/src/main.ts:18:5)
```

Sample 17.3: Example stack trace

As you can see, the error message and stack trace can tell a developer what problem occurred and let them find the source of the error by seeing each line of code that was involved in the error.

TypeScript function declarations unfortunately don't support describing potential thrown Errors, but they can be described using JSDoc comments, a standard for writing code comments in JavaScript:

Resulting TypeScript Function Definition

```
/**
 * Converts a string to a number.
 * @param {string} input The string to convert.
 * @returns {number} The converted number.
 * @throws {Error} Throws error if input is not a valid number.
 */
const stringToNumber = (input: string) => number;
```

Sample 17.4: Function declaration for a function that can throw an error

JSI Implementation

In JavaScript Native Interface, there is a `facebook::jsi::JSError` object which receives a `std::string` as a parameter during construction.

C++

```
JSError jsError = JSError(
    runtime,
    "Explanation of error message"
);
```

Sample 17.5: Creating a JavaScript-compatible Error in JSI

There are two ways to pass the Error back to TypeScript. One method is by using the runtime.throwException() function:

C++

```
runtime.throwException(JSError(
    runtime,
    "Explanation of error message"
));
```

Sample 17.6: Using the throwException() function to throw an Error

The other method is to simply throw it, as you would any other native exception:

C++

```
throw JSError(
    runtime,
    "Explanation of error message"
);
```

Sample 17.7: Throwing a JavaScript Error

If we are catching native errors, we can use the exception.what() method to get the Exception description when creating the JSError, for example:

C++

```
try {
  int x = 100 / 0;
} catch (std::exception& exception) {
  throw JSError(
    runtime,
    exception.what()
  );
}
```

Sample 17.9: Converting native exceptions to JSErrors

Example: String To Number Function

In the `stringToNumber()` function described earlier in the chapter, we try to convert a `string` into a number and throw an `Error` if the result is not a valid number or there was some other problem in the conversion.

C++

```
Function stringToNumber = Function::createFromHostFunction(...{
  // casting as string fails if `arguments[0]` isn't a string
  string input = arguments[0].getString(runtime).utf8(runtime);
  try {
    return Value(std::stod(input));
  } catch (const std::invalid_argument& e) {
    // Error: input is not a valid number
    throw JSError(
      runtime,
      "Input string is not a valid number"
    );
  } catch (const std::out_of_range& e) {
    // Error: result is out of range for a double
    throw JSError(
      runtime,
      "Number is out of range"
    );
  }
});
```

Example 17.1: Implementing a function that throws Errors

In TypeScript there is no way to declare that a function can throw an error, so we can only define the function name, parameters, and return type:

TypeScript

```
declare global {
    function stringToNumber(param: string): number;
}
```

Sample 17.10: Declaring a JSI function in TypeScript

In TypeScript, we call this method as we would any other. We can use a try / catch block to handle any possible errors and print them to the console or ideally provide the user with actionable feedback:

TypeScript

```
try {
    const number = stringToNumber("Hello");
    console.log(number);
} catch (error: any) {
    console.error(error.message);
    console.error(error.stack);
}
```

Sample 17.11: Calling JSI stringToNumber() function with error handling

Appendix I: JSI Data Types

Array - a list or collection of data

Boolean - a single-bit, `true` / `false` or `0` / `1` value

Null - a value an empty assignment.

Function - callable unit of code which can be executed by another part of the program.

Number - any numeric value including integers such as `123` or `-123` or floating point numbers such as `1.23` or `-1.23`.

Object - a structured data which contains named values and functions

Promise - an object which can execute a callback or throw an error after an unknown time delay.

String - an object containing a sequence of characters and properties such as `.length` and several functions. JavaScript strings are assumed to be UTF-8 compatible.

Undefined - a value which has not been assigned.

Value - a generic data type which can represent any of boolean, array, number, string, object, null, function, or unknown.

Appendix II: Glossary

ASCII - a character encoding scheme which supports up to 255 characters due to its 8-bit encoding of characters. Typically used to represent latin letters (a-z and A-Z) and numbers 0-9.

Argument - data that is passed into a function at runtime.

Array - a linear collection or list of data.

Callback - a function that is passed as an argument to another function, so it can be called after some time has passed or an event has been triggered.

Java - A bytecode-compiled language which has sophisticated object handling and type checking.

JSDoc - A standard style of block comment in JavaScript

Java Native Interface (JNI) - a feature of Java that can execute binary code.

JavaScript - A programming language invented to program web pages, but now runs on desktop and mobile devices.

JavaScript Native Interface (JSI) - a feature of React Native JavaScript which can execute binary code.

Lambda - An nameless function that gets called on-the-fly by another function.

Object - A data structure which contains addressable values.

Parameter - the expected argument type(s) defined to be passed into a function.

Pointer - a memory address where an array, object, or other data structure can be found.

React - A JavaScript framework for building web pages.

React Native - a cross-platform mobile and desktop app development language that is coded in TypeScript or JavaScript

Reference - a way of passing structured data such as objects or arrays to a function so that the object can be accessed directly.

Thread - a sequential execution of code.

TypeScript - An extension of JavaScript which adds type-hinting and validation to variables and functions.

UTF-8 - a character encoding that uses 8-bit ASCII encoding for latin letters (a-z and A-Z) and numbers 0-9, but 16-bit encoding for accent characters and foreign language glyphs.

Appendix II: Glossary

About the Author

Tony is an open source contributor to the react-native-libsodium project and the PKT Blockchain. His curiosity compels him to want to open up and understand everything he touches so he can share that understanding with others.

He has two true passions: branding and inventing.

His passion for branding led him to start a company that did branding and marketing in four countries for firms such as Apple, Intel, and Sony BMG. He loves weaving the elements of design, writing, product, and strategy into an essential truth that defines a company.

His passion for inventing led him to start a company that uses brain imaging to quantify meditation and to predict seizures, which acquired $1.5m in funding and was incubated in San Francisco where he currently resides.

Those same passions have led him on some adventures as well, including living in a Greek monastery with orthodox monks and tagging along with a busker in Spain to learn how to play flamenco guitar.

About this Book

In mobile development, there is a trade-off between portability code and fast execution. A new feature of React Native called JavaScript Native Interface (JSI) removes that trade-off by allowing developers to write portable code that executes as binary code on the native device.

What You Will Learn

This book teaches you how to write JSI code so that you can have write-once, run-everywhere mobile apps that feel like they are written in native code.

You will learn how to set up a JSI project on MacOS, Windows, and Linux. It will teach you how to register native functions, and how to accept any type of parameter and return any type of value. Importantly, this also includes working with objects, arrays, callback functions, and promises.

Who This Book Is For

This book is intended for programmers, engineers, and technology enthusiasts who want to learn about mobile development.

Related Books

If you want to learn about how to implement a REST API, how to use HTTP verbs, JSON data structures, URIs, and HTTP error codes properly in your REST APIs' check out my book, *Learn Rest APIs*.

eBook ISBN: 978-1-9993817-8-3
Paperback ISBN: 978-1-989775-00-4

backupbrain.co/titles/learn-rest-apis

If you want to learn how to create ultra-secure login workflows where the user's password never leaves their device, check out my book, OPAQUE

backupbrain.co/titles/opaque

eBook ISBN: 978-1-989775-17-2
Paperback ISBN: 978-1-989775-16-5

www.ingramcontent.com/pod-product-compliance
Lightning Source LLC
La Vergne TN
LVHW022311060326
832902LV00020B/3395